PERSONAL FINANCE FOR YOUNG ADULTS

FROM BROKE TO BOSS 7 SIMPLE STEPS TO BUILDING
WEALTH, CRUSHING DEBT, AND LIVING YOUR BEST
LIFE AS A FINANCIAL BEGINNER

KIRK TEACHOUT

IV QUARTER
PUBLISHING

CONTENTS

INTRODUCTION

> "College graduates spent 16 years gaining skills that will help them command a higher salary; yet little or no time is spent helping them save, invest and grow their money."
>
> — VINCE SHORB, CEO OF THE NATIONAL FINANCIAL EDUCATORS COUNCIL

When you graduate from high school (and college, for that matter), adults often say things like "the world is your oyster!" or "this is going to be an exciting new chapter in your life!" Your parents might have said these things with enthusiasm — sparkles twinkling in their eyes — while hugging you after your graduation, perhaps not remembering how scary life can be for a new adult.

At this point, you were probably feeling the excitement as well. Graduating from high school or college *is* a big deal, after all! Graduating from high school in particular is a milestone that marks the beginning of adulthood. A lot of 18-year-olds are understandably hyped to move out of their parent's house, get their own apartment, and attend college.

At this age, you feel more than ready to spread your wings and set out on your own. Despite this, however, you can feel a pit growing in the bottom of your stomach. "Why is rent so expensive?" You mutter to yourself while looking through apartment listings online. "How on Earth am I going to pay my college tuition? When will I even have time to work?"

Upon entering adulthood, most people realize just how unbelievably expensive everything is. There are rent and utility bills to pay. For college students in particular, there are textbooks, groceries, on-campus parking, car insurance, health insurance, doctor's appointments, and dentist appointments to pay for. Not to mention the cost of college tuition. It's enough to make you feel sick to your stomach, which is why most people don't like thinking about it.

This stuff tends to build up, though, like a snowball rolling down a hill. "Just get a credit card," people will tell you, but that can be a dangerous line to walk. If you're relying on a credit card to pay for most of your expenses, you may run into trouble later in life. For instance, take the story of Amanda Chatel, who had to file for bankruptcy at the age of 23.

As an 18-year-old, Amanda decided to get a credit card without telling her parents about it. Her father had always warned her about the risks that come with credit cards, but as a new adult, Amanda felt compelled to make her own choice regarding the matter. The credit card company lured her in with talk of "building credit" and "learning responsibility." The idea of having access to invisible funds was enough to eventually win her over.

She began to spend her credit card money on things like shoes, clothes, and taking her friends out to lunch. All she had to do was pay it back eventually, right? It was no big deal. By the time she was a sophomore in college, however, she had two credit cards and was thousands of dollars in debt. Things continued to snowball from there, and by the time she graduated from college, she had racked up about $25,000 in credit card debt. Not only that, but she had to worry about paying back her college loans. Talk about over-whelming!

Eventually, she had no choice but to file for bankruptcy — meaning she wouldn't be allowed to have a credit card for the next seven years. She realized this was probably for the best considering how irresponsible she'd been with her money, but filing for bankruptcy obviously wasn't ideal. She took a massive hit on her credit score, which probably made it exceptionally difficult for her to do things like rent an apartment or lease a car.

If you're a young adult who's currently struggling with finances, just know that you're not alone. Many adults (including myself) have been in your shoes. Being neck-deep in debt can feel like the end of the world, but don't worry. There are ways to slowly dig yourself out of this debt, and there are also ways to avoid generating too much debt for yourself in the first place. You can easily avoid what happened to Amanda and many other young adults like her, as long as you have the right information on hand.

A lot of young people struggle so much with finances because they never learned how to incorporate healthy financial habits. For whatever reason, this isn't some-thing they teach you in high school (although, it really should be). Most young people end up mimicking their parents when it comes to financial habits. Even if they watched their parents struggle with money while growing up, it's the only example they have to base their own financial habits.

Contrary to popular belief, many young people *aren't* frivolous with their money. However, even those with healthy spending habits can run into trouble at times. Plenty of young people are aware that they weren't taught anything about managing their finances in high school, which, naturally, is pretty anxiety-inducing. The future is also quite uncertain, so young people have to worry about how the current state of the economy are going to impact their financial well-being.

What is the answer, then? Work yourself to death? A lot of young people probably watched their parents do this, and — noticing how miserable they were all the time — don't want to do the same thing. Most Generation Z adults are looking for ways to work smarter, not harder these days. They want to actually enjoy their lives, rather than work until they drop.

Many Gen Z adults also dream of a luxurious lifestyle. Compared to millennials and Gen X, around 23% of Gen Z adults have stated that being famous is important to them. This makes sense, considering the number of influencers and celebrities they see living it up on social media apps like Instagram and TikTok. It's perfectly normal for people to see others living a lavish lifestyle and think: "I want that, too." Many Gen Z adults (and older adults as well) don't understand how influencers can afford to live this type of lifestyle. Social media often hides the fact that influencers have wealthy parents or that they are actually in debt themselves.

It took me a long time to learn financial literacy, and I wouldn't have got where I am today without the help I received along the way. That's why I'm here to help you! I've been exactly where you are, financially, and I know just how scary it can be to watch your debts build up. Any fears you have about the future are completely valid. The world is ever-changing, and you only get one life! You should get to live your life the way you want to, without worrying about financial issues getting in the way.

It may take some time and effort to gain momentum toward your financial goals, but one of the best pieces of advice I can give you right now is this: start early. Those who are able to save as much as they can while also managing their spending habits as young adults will be more likely to have a healthy wallet when they reach older adulthood. By reading this book, you can learn how to avoid digging yourself into a pit of debt and eventually achieve financial literacy. By writing this book, I aim to educate young adults like you on how to set yourself up for future financial success.

You'll finally get an opportunity to deep dive into the things you should have learned in high school — such as the importance of becoming financially literate, as well as how being financially literate can help you avoid debt, build your wealth, live the life you want to live, and maybe even retire early. What you decide to focus on determines your self-growth. If you take the time to sit down and focus on growing your knowledge about money and what you're going to go through in order to become financially literate, you'll eventually succeed. Achieving your financial goals won't be easy, but it's certainly possible to work towards these goals if you have the right tools and information on hand. Let's get started, shall we?

1

IT ALL STARTS WITH YOUR MINDSET

When it comes to managing your finances (and anything in life, really), your mindset can make a huge difference. A lot of young people have trouble thinking logically about money and developing healthy spending habits, especially those of us who aren't particularly good with numbers. Many young people who are new to the working world will feel like they've got their financial situation under control, but only right after they've gotten paid. "I just got paid, so it's okay if I make this big purchase" is certainly a phrase I said on more than one occasion while in my early twenties. I also remember having to live on instant ramen at the end of each month; just barely scraping by until I got my next paycheck.

Does this sound familiar? When you enter the work-force and start earning biweekly paychecks, it can feel like a whole new world. Suddenly having money to spend can make it hard for some young people to keep things in perspective. When I was 18, I worked at a pizza place while living at my mom's house. The idea was that I would live there while saving up money to move out and get my own apartment, but this proved to be more difficult than I had originally anticipated.

Because I didn't have to pay rent at my mom's house, I had money to spend for the first time in my life. I'd go out to dinner with my friends all the time, and make frankly outrageous purchases on things like clothes, video games, and coffee to go. Needless to say, these things added up. My mom began to say things like: "how much money have you saved up?" and "how's the apartment hunting going?" It made me nervous. It made me feel bad — like I was a burden on her because I didn't know how to be responsible with my money.

It's worth mentioning, at this point, that you're not entirely to blame for your financial difficulties. But, I do want you to take ownership of your decisions. The world can be a harsh place. Gas prices are through the roof, and inflation has never been this high. Your parents might not realize that the cost of living is significantly higher than it was when they were your age. Meanwhile, the minimum wage in most places has hardly increased at all.

It's not productive to blame absolutely everything on the system, but I'm not going to deny the fact that the system is broken. With how expensive everything is now, it's no wonder that young people are having such a difficult time staying afloat. When you're financially illiterate in a system that doesn't really work all that well, you're going to struggle. Obviously, this is terrible, but gaining financial literacy is easier than most people think it is.

The important thing is that you start learning financial literacy early, while you're still young and relatively free of debt. You have a lot of untapped financial potential; it's just a matter of digging deep and making the right financial moves as a young person. The earlier you're able to adopt this mindset, the sooner you'll be able to start living your life on your own terms! Let's take a look at this statement from the University of Central Florida financial aid website:

"Developing and maintaining healthy spending habits can greatly impact your financial future. Overspending can lead to a lack of available funds when the unexpected occurs. Developing a spending plan helps you to understand what monetary resources are available to you as well as your expected expenses." Now see, this is what I'm talking about when I say becoming financially literate requires adopting a healthy mindset around money and spending!

When coming up with a suitable spending plan for yourself, you should always prioritize your needs. It's a good idea to put aside money for things like rent, utility bills, food, and emergencies. Making sure that these necessities are taken care of will ensure that you won't have to dig between the couch cushions for spare change when your landlord comes knocking to collect your rent check.

So, that's what a significant portion of your paycheck will go to: your necessities. The rest of your money should go to your savings and your wants (i.e. going out to eat, a new pair of shoes, etc.) Just be conscientious about how much you spend on your wants. If you're spending so much that you don't have anything left to put in your savings account, then you're heading into financially irresponsible territory. This is not to say that you shouldn't treat yourself once in a while. Just like anything else, spending money on what you want (but don't need) should be done in moderation.

FINANCIAL ISSUES YOUNG ADULTS FACE

Many young adults are accustomed to relying on their parents when it comes to dealing with financial matters. Some parents even help their adult children through college and graduate school, which while gracious, can certainly slow the rate at which these young adults are able to learn financial literacy and proper money management. There are four main hurdles young adults typically have to overcome when they enter the working world. Let's take a look at these hurdles below:

Paying Off Student Loans

Most young people don't even like to *think* about their student loans. This is understandable, considering student loans are one of the most stressful things most people have to deal with throughout their entire lifetimes. Saddling an 18-year-old with $20,000 in debt feels a bit cruel, to be honest, but that's just the way the higher education system works right now.

For most people, their student loan debt is only continuing to grow. More and more young adults these days are seeking Master's degrees as well, which only adds to their student debt. A lot of people feel like they have no other choice, though. Having a Bachelor's degree just doesn't seem to cut it anymore for most high-paying jobs out there.

Learning Financial Illiteracy

Because financial literacy is typically not taught in schools, millennials and Gen Z adults often have to take initiative and educate themselves. It's difficult to know *how* to educate yourself on financial literacy, though, which is why most young adults end up learning about it the hard way (like Amanda Chatel, for example).

When you grow up and move out of your parents' house, you suddenly have a lot to juggle financially. Dealing with student loans and paying your rent and bills on time each month is only a small part of it. It's totally possible for any young adult to learn financial literacy, but as I said, it's a lot like juggling. Becoming financially literate takes time and practice, and you'll occasionally drop a ball or two. And that's okay.

Investing and Taking Risks

Considering the economy's lack of stability during the Great Recession, it's no surprise that millennials and Gen Z adults are afraid of investing in the stock market. Most have likely heard stories from their parents of investments going poorly, and some have

PERSONAL FINANCE FOR YOUNG ADULTS | 21

probably even seen their parents' stock investment returns disappear into thin air. Despite a few rough years, the stock market *has* made money. Young adults, however, have gotten the fear of losing money to an investment deeply ingrained within their minds.

The fact of the matter is, making investments is not well understood by young adults. There's a certain amount of risk that goes into it, but the payout is often worth this risk. According to the CFP and wealth manager at Ford Financial Group, Brian Ullmann, younger investors tend to "have a much lower tolerance for risk." Those who are unwilling to take risks when making an investment are unlikely to see any major payout from said investment. This unfortunately means that young people end up missing out on a lot of great opportunities.

Feeling Pressured to Follow a Worn-out Path

As a young adult, you've probably had a baby boomer give you unsolicited advice about financial planning before. The only problem with the advice people from older generations give younger generations is that the world is vastly different from how it was when these people were your age. I was just speaking with a friend about this the other day. She told me about how her dad is still working full-time at the age of 71 because he can't afford to retire. Why can't he afford to retire, you might ask? Well, it's at least partly because the cost of living has gotten so expensive and he didn't make proper financial decisions during adulthood!

A person in their seventies would have had a lot less trouble surviving on social security benefits alone "back in the day," although, the system has never been perfect. Ideally, you should be able to save up for your retirement, but this can end up being more difficult than most people anticipate. A lot of young people can't see that far ahead into the future, and life happens, you know? There comes a time when you get married, buy a house, and have babies (if you want to) and all of that is relatively expensive.

For this reason, most younger millennials and Gen Z adults are waiting longer to get married and have kids. They're choosing to rent apartments for most of their lives, perhaps because they've seen what can happen when someone has all of their money tied up in a house. This is actually a perfectly fine way to live, as long as you're happy. Older generations won't necessarily understand it because it's an altered version of the American Dream, but most feel like "the American Dream" is past-due for some editing, anyway.

Short-term Thinking vs. Long-term Vision

As a young person, you're often thinking about the short-term rather than the long-term. The problem with this is that short-term thinkers tend to focus solely on instant gratification. They don't always consider the consequences that their spending habits could have on their future. People who have a long-term vision, however, are always thinking ahead. They're concerned about what might happen months or even years from the present, and their spending habits reflect that way of thinking.

It's important to note that thinking short-term and having a long-term vision for your finances is not black and white. You can do both at the same time, and even develop a healthy balance between the two as long as you're financially literate. It's worth mentioning, however, that too much short-term thinking oftentimes ends in failure, while those who prioritize their long-term visions tend to have greater success in life — both financially and otherwise.

As an example, let's take a look at the spending habits of two different hypothetical individuals: a millennial named Kate, and a Gen Z adult named Darren. Kate, being a bit older, learned to develop an outcome-oriented mindset. After going through a messy divorce, she realized that she needed to take a step back and evaluate her life. She began saving up money for her retirement, knowing that doing so would significantly benefit her later on.

Darren, on the other hand, was constantly blowing his paycheck on things like takeout and video games. Because he was crashing on a wealthy friend's couch, he didn't think he'd have to worry about saving up his money for things like rent, utilities, emergencies, or his retirement. He even bought himself a new computer, which — although he didn't really need it — gave him instant gratification. By the time Darren and Kate reached old age, Darren found that he had to work sixty hours a week just to get by. Kate, on the other hand, was able to settle down in a nice big farmhouse with her new husband.

I'm not saying this is exactly the way things always pan out, but you can see how much difference having a long-term vision can make for your financial, mental, and emotional health. It's often challenging for young people to follow through on their long-term plans, because, as I said, life happens. The problem is, life will always happen. Unfortunately, if you have the mindset that you have to dip into your savings account every time "life happens," you'll never be able to break your bad financial habits and actually save money.

Also, instant gratification feels really, really nice. It goes without saying that the reason for this inability to follow through stems from an inability to see yourself as an older adult. When I was in my early twenties, I couldn't imagine what it would be like to be 35, let alone 65.

Part of the problem is, no young person likes the idea of giving up on dreams that could provide them with instant gratification just so they can save long-term for something that feels far away. There's a tendency to romanticize "living in the moment," and hey, living in the moment is definitely important in its own way. Most young adults just need to figure out a good balance between living in the moment and investing in their future.

BUILDING YOUR FINANCIAL MINDSET

If you've developed a negative mindset around money due to bad past experiences with things like debt and bankruptcy, you're certainly not alone. Not having money is stressful, and a lot of young people find themselves simultaneously hating money while also wanting and needing it. I think a lot of us wish society was less money-focused, but for now, money does (in a way) buy happiness. Or, at the very least, money buys comfort and a sense of security. As the saying goes: "money can't buy happiness, but it's more comfortable to cry in a luxury car than on a bicycle."

So, let's talk about how you can start building a healthy financial mindset. Thinking about money in a positive way will ultimately help you make more of it, save more of it, and invest more of it into your future. If you're having trouble wrapping your mind around the concept of building a good mindset around money, here's what you can do:

Gain an Understanding of Your Thoughts and Emotions Surrounding Money

Consider this scene from Louise Fitzhugh's young adult novel *Harriet the Spy*: while talking to her best friend, Sport, 11-year-old Harriet says "I hate money." Sport, who comes from a low-income family says "well, you'd jolly well like it if you didn't have any." What Harriet says about money comes from a place of privilege, while Sport's mindset is born from being underprivileged. Both characters have unhealthy emotions surrounding money, and this is because money is so complicated while also being so very needed.

If you've never really had to think about money, you're probably benefitting from some sort of privilege. The word "privilege" has unfortunately developed a negative connotation in recent years, but it's not actually a bad thing. To have privilege simply means to have an advantage compared to others as a result of certain circumstances. If you do benefit from privilege, you might as well take advantage of it — as you should with every opportunity life throws at you.

Even if you benefit from privilege, you might still have some complex feelings about money. For a day, try writing down your thoughts and emotions after making purchases. At the end of the day, look over what you've written with an open mind. What brought you joy when you bought it? What brought you guilt? What brought you both? This is a great way to evaluate your spending habits and eventually shift your mindset around money.

Stop Comparing Yourself to Others

Have you ever logged onto Instagram and started feeling bad about yourself? Perhaps your friend from high school shared a post about getting married and buying her first house, or maybe that guy who used to bully you in middle school is a successful CEO of some big company now. I won't argue with the fact that life can be unfair, but you must remember this: social media is a lie.

When people post on Instagram, Snapchat, and TikTok, they're typically sharing the best parts of their lives while omitting the bad parts. This can create the illusion that life is nothing but great for some people, but that's just not the case. For example, your old friend from high school might be sharing pictures of herself living the high life every weekend, but she could literally be neck-deep in credit card debt. The truth is, you just don't know!

Forgive Yourself for Financial Mistakes You Made in the Past

Amanda Chatel never would have gotten to where she is now if she hadn't forgiven herself for the financial mistakes she made in her early twenties. Most people make bad financial choices at some point in their lives. For example, maybe you went out to eat too many times and spent more money than you meant to on an expensive meal. It happens to the best of us, and it's important to forgive yourself rather than beat yourself up about it.

As human beings, we progress through our lives by learning from our mistakes. This especially goes for young adults like you. Try to keep in mind that the human brain doesn't fully develop until the age of 25. It's *okay* to make mistakes sometimes, and hey, at the time, those financial mistakes made you happy. The past is in the past. What's important is what you decide to do now that you've gained some financial literacy.

Form Good Spending Habits

It takes time and work to develop healthy spending habits, but don't worry. You'll get there. It's a good idea to set aside some time each week to go over your bills and consider areas in your life where you can cut down on your spending. Remember to set realistic goals for yourself, and don't be afraid to save and invest for your future. Start small, and keep going. Once you're able to form better spending habits, you'll certainly notice a difference in your bank account.

Create a Good Budget for Yourself

It can be difficult to stick to a budget, especially if you're used to living a relatively expensive lifestyle. A lot of people feel like budgets can be limiting — a buzzkill — but this doesn't have to be the case. If you want, you can start by giving yourself a loose budget. That way, you'll have some wiggle room if you want to treat yourself to a nice dinner once in a while. In general, when it comes to dividing up your money, you should try to put at least half of your monthly income towards necessities, like rent and bills. Try to put twenty percent of your money into a savings account, or use it to pay off your debts. The money you have left after that can be your spending money. We'll go over this in more detail in a later chapter.

Be Thankful for What You Have

When you're stressing out about money, it can be helpful to take a step back and put things into perspective. Yes, you live in a tiny apartment, but at least you have a roof over your head. Yes, you may be surviving on ramen and cheese quesadillas, but at least you won't go hungry. It's important that you don't obsess over money or let it control you in any way. Money is crucial for survival, but you don't want to spend all your time thinking about it. Be thankful for all that you have, and worry about making more money later. It's all going to be okay.

INTERACTIVE ELEMENT

Feeling confident about developing a more healthy financial mindset? Practice your skills with this short quiz:

1. What should you do if you want to develop a good financial mindset? (Circle all that apply)

    a. Figure out your feelings surrounding money
    b. Create a weekly or monthly budget

c. Complain about money to your parents

d. Forgive yourself for financial mistakes you made in the past

2. Which statements are true about financial wants and financial needs?

a. Financial wants are essential and financial needs are optional

b. Financial wants and needs are the same thing

c. Financial wants are optional and financial needs are essential

d. Financial needs should be prioritized over financial wants

3. What are some examples of financial needs?

a. Rent

b. Bills

c. A pair of fancy shoes

d. Dentist appointments

4. Why should you create a budget?

a. It will help you save money

b. It will help you keep track of your expenses

c. It will help you plan for the long-term

d. It will ensure that you'll always have money on hand

Answer Key:

1. a), b), and d)
2. c) and d)
3. a), b), and d)
4. All of the above

SEGUE

Becoming financially literate is all about taking the correct action steps. By coming up with challenging yet achievable goals for yourself, you'll be able to increase your chances of setting yourself up for financial success. In the next chapter, I'll dive into how you can set reasonable financial goals for yourself, as well as continue to stick to them despite all that life throws your way.

2

ACTION STEP 1: SET FINANCIAL GOALS

Why is goal setting such an important part of the financial planning process? Most people set goals in all areas of their life, whether they're aware of it or not. You probably have goals for your romantic life (i.e. "I'm going to be a more present partner"), or for your work life (i.e. "I'm going to meet my sales quota"). It only makes sense to set goes for your financial life as well! How should you go about setting financial goals for yourself? Well, the first thing you're going to want to do is to define your financial pain points.

Setting financial goals is ultimately all about planning for the long term. Consider this statement from *The Economic Times*: "Setting of goals marks the beginning of financial planning to help you achieve the objectives at various life stages. Goal-setting gives meaning and direction to the various financial decisions you will take during your lifetime." Having a sense of meaning and direction in your life (financially or otherwise) is crucial. It's a basic human need, just like getting a good night's sleep or eating a hearty meal.

At one point or another, you've probably said or have heard someone say: "I don't know what I'm doing with my life." This difficult crisis is often born from a lack of goals. Without goals, you'll have a hard time determining which way is up and which way is down. You'll be stumbling around in the dark, grasping for purpose, when the purpose is really meant to come from within you. Goals and purpose are directly linked. You've got to determine your own purpose by creating goals and sticking to them. Otherwise, you risk getting lost in the darkness.

Those who don't set financial goals are also more likely to find themselves getting into financial trouble. It's a great way to stay organized and keep track of your finances, as well as develop a sense of financial purpose. In this chapter, I'll do a deep dive into why setting financial goals is so important, how to effectively set financial goals, and the mistakes you should avoid when setting financial goals for yourself.

WHY YOU SHOULD SET FINANCIAL GOALS

Everyone wants to feel financially secure, but this is oftentimes easier said than done. Financial security isn't something that just *happens* to you one day. Even people who win the lottery have to go through the process of getting the lottery ticket and checking the numbers. These people are also *extremely* lucky. Most people lose money by playing the lottery, so that's not a road you want to go down.

There are plenty of reasons why you should set financial goals. For example, let's say you want to move out of your parent's house and start renting your own apartment. Naturally, you'll want to consider all of the action steps that need to take place between Point A and Point B. Just sort of vaguely saving your money whenever you can isn't going to cut it, especially if you're dipping into your savings account every other week for non-necessities!

Setting financial goals is all about knowing how to visualize timeframes. When doing assignments for school or work, you're typically required to complete a certain amount of work within a certain amount of time. Working on a deadline and learning how to divide up your work into multiple days helps you hone your time management skills, which is why high school teachers and college professors tend to assign big projects several weeks in advance.

Like with school and work, procrastinating and doing things in a disorganized way can end up hurting you when it comes to managing your financials. Spending your money all willy-nilly is essentially the same thing as winging an assignment the day before it's due. You'll probably be okay in the end, but at what cost? All of the stress and effort you put into rushing the assignment (or, in this case, scrounging for loose change) won't be worth it in the end. All you'll have left after the fact is empty pockets and a mediocre grade.

So, let's take some time to go over why setting financial goals are so important. It may be difficult to picture your financial goals at first, but visualizing them will get easier over time, especially if you consider the factors listed below:

Direction

It's important to keep in mind that you're not saving and investing money for no reason. When it comes to sticking to your financial goals, you've got to keep your eyes on the prize. If you decide you want to stick to a weekly or monthly budget, for example, you should make this an actual goal for yourself. Thinking of your financial wants and needs as goals will help you stick to your plans because you know exactly what outcome you're striving for. Nobody wants to fail at their goals, after all. Having set financial goals can help you stay pointed in the right direction as you walk through life and improve upon your spending habits.

Accountability

One of the best things you can do for your financial health is to start holding yourself accountable for your financial actions. Write down all of your financial goals in one place. This way, when you mess up, you can't make excuses by saying "I forgot." You *know* you have goals you want and need to stick to, and being financially responsible is a big part of being responsible for your own happiness and well-being. I'm not saying you should beat yourself up when you make financial mistakes, but don't think that you can't be held accountable either. When you mess up, learn from it, review your list of goals and say: "I may have messed up, but here's how I can avoid messing up again in the future."

Motivation

Setting financial goals shouldn't feel like a drag. The whole point of setting goals is to stay motivated and ultimately improve your life. As I said before, keep your eyes on the prize. Figure out what's most important to you and create specific, realistic goals that make you excited about what's to come should you successfully achieve these goals. When the going gets tough, keep your goals in mind. No matter what happens, you've got to grit your teeth and stay motivated. Your future is important, after all!

Accomplishment

One of the main reasons people set goals is because having a sense of accomplishment feels great. Accomplishing something can pull you out of a difficult crisis and make you feel whole again, especially if you've been going through a rough time lately. When setting financial goals, you should also set milestones for yourself. When you reach a certain milestone, reward yourself with something fun! You certainly deserve it.

HOW TO SET EFFECTIVE FINANCIAL GOALS

Consider what you want your future to be like. What are your dreams and aspirations? Do you want to have your own house someday? Do you want to be able to send your future children to college? Perhaps you dream of traveling the world someday, but with the way things are going right now, that doesn't feel financially plausible. I'm here to tell you that all of these things are financially plausible, as long as you're willing to set and stick to your financial goals.

Even if you are great with organization and can keep things together in your head, I recommend putting your goals into writing. Setting financial goals is a lot like eating an extravagant wedding cake or playing a game of Jenga. If you start from the bottom, you're likely to end up with a huge mess. To use another analogy, your financial goals are essentially like the branches growing off of one big financial tree. This tree may be "early retirement," and the branches growing off of it could be: "save money," "stick to a budget," and "pay off your debts on time."

It's up to you to decide which branches you want to climb first. A big part of financial planning is determining which financial goals you want to prioritize. With that being said, let's discuss the recommended steps you should take when setting financial goals for yourself.

Prioritize

The importance of prioritizing and organizing your financial goals cannot be stressed enough! I highly recommend separating your financial goals into two different categories: your wants and your needs. As much as you feel like you *need* a new car or a trip to Paris, these things are actually wants! You need to learn how to prioritize the things that are going to keep you alive and financially secure. Financial needs include things like groceries, being able to pay rent and utility bills, and having a comfortable retirement.

In terms of paying for things like living expenses and bills from doctor's appointments or trips to the emergency room, it's a good idea to build up an emergency fund. Your emergency fund should be a financial priority for you as well, because you never know what could happen. Just to be clear, I'm not saying buying a new car or taking a trip to Paris *shouldn't* be on your list of goals. I'm simply trying to stress the fact that these things should be relatively low on your list of priorities. It might take some time, but you'll get there. Don't worry about it too much.

Get Specific with Your Goals

Once you get your priorities in order, the next thing you'll want to do is determine what achieving your financial goals will require. It may be beneficial to assign a specific price tag to each of your financial goals. For example, if one of your goals is to save up an emergency fund, you should try to figure out exactly how much money you want to put into that fund. Let's say you want to save up $5,000 for emergency living expenses. It's a good idea to set a micro-goal for yourself in this case, such as putting $200 into your savings account every time you get your paycheck.

You should also try to set deadlines for yourself. Figure out when exactly you'll need a specific amount of money, and for what. To stay organized, write this information down. It could be helpful to separate your money into short-term, medium-term, and long-term funds. Your short-term funds are what you need right now (i.e. money for groceries and rent). Your medium-term funds might be for things like doctor's appointments or taking your car to the mechanic. Your long-term funds are what you'll eventually use for your future home, your kids' college expenses, and your retirement.

Take Action

Now that you've determined your financial goals and the amount of savings you'll need to complete each goal, you can incorporate your goals into one big comprehensive financial plan. When writing out this plan, you should consider both your current circumstances and your future aspirations. I previously mentioned the importance of starting early when it comes to financial planning. The earlier you're able to start saving money, the better!

You should also keep in mind that your goals may end up changing as you ride the wave of life. If you get married and start having babies, that could significantly change the way you think about money. You might need to alter your goals and priorities to better fit your new lifestyle, which is perfectly valid. This is another reason why it's important to save as much money as you can while you're still young. You never know what life is going to throw at you, but having the ability to be flexible and adaptable with your funds should alleviate some of the stress you're likely to face.

MISTAKES TO AVOID

A friend of mine recently checked his bank account and discovered that he had accumulated a frightening amount of negative money. He ended up having to ask his parents to help him so that he could afford rent. "How did you let this happen?" his dad asked him, obviously upset. My friend, at the time, wasn't even sure what had happened, but after a quick call with his bank, he discovered that he'd forgotten about his subscriptions and bills that had been set for automatic payment.

A big part of his problem (though, he had trouble initially admitting this) was that his income didn't match the lifestyle he was trying to live. He started searching things online like "where to donate plasma" and "how to make money fast," not wanting to forego his weekly trips to the city or the expensive dinner date he had planned with his girlfriend for Valentine's day. He soon realized, though, that there were some things he needed to give up if he didn't want to end up with negative money in his checking account every month.

It can be challenging to avoid making financial mistakes, especially if these mistakes stem from the financial goals you've set. If you have the right information, however, making financial mistakes is totally avoidable. Listed below are some of the most common mistakes young people make when setting financial goals:

Setting Goals Based Only on Your Current Lifestyle

Although instant gratification feels nice, it's not actually your friend — especially when you're trying to be financially responsible. It's only natural to want to improve your immediate circumstances when setting financial goals for yourself, but it's important to keep your future in mind as well. At the moment, you might be saving a bit of money each month just to stay afloat, but this will ultimately only benefit you for the short term. Consider where you'll be in twenty, thirty, or even fifty years and start a savings account based on those particular lifestyle accommodations.

Setting Too Many Goals at Once

Setting financial goals is important and necessary, but you don't want to overwhelm yourself by setting too many goals at once. You might be tempted to set a lot of big, expensive goals for yourself, but this is not a good idea. You're going to want to start by setting goals that are achievable. Remember to be patient with yourself as you're adjusting to living by your new financial goals, and don't bite off more than you can chew.

Ignoring Inflation

Inflation is incredibly high right now, and that's definitely something to take into consideration. As you work towards your financial goals, you might start to realize just how much inflation is impacting your ability to achieve what you want to achieve. You might find that some months, you can't put as much money into your savings account as you would have liked to, and that's okay. These things take time, and it's important to keep a level head. Chances are, you'll need to save more money than you think you do. This may require cutting some subscriptions, such as Netflix and Spotify, for a while until you're able to afford them.

Not Distinguishing Between Wants and Needs

Again, prioritizing your financial goals is key. You might want to take a vacation to the Bahamas or use what's already in your savings account to buy a new car, but these things aren't as important as saving up to build an emergency fund. It's important to look at the big picture when coming up with your financial plan. There's a certain amount of romanticization around the concept of living fast and dying young, but this mindset isn't exactly healthy, is it? Decide what you need most, and what you want most, and prioritize these things accordingly.

Forgetting About Your Annual Expenses

As a young adult, it can be difficult to juggle all of your monthly and yearly expenses. Your phone bill, car insurance, and mortgage payments all need to be factored into your monthly budget. These things can be expensive, and they can sneak up on you if you're not careful. It's also important to remember to set aside money for things like healthcare, dental care, and car maintenance. Try to keep your annual expenses in order as well. The last thing you want to do is be caught off guard by an unexpected charge to your bank account.

INTERACTIVE ELEMENT

- Prioritizing your financial goals can help you figure out what's truly important. This involves distinguishing between your wants and needs. Your needs (rent expenses, emergency money, etc.) should be at the top of your list. Your wants (new clothes, travel funds) should be relatively low on your list of priorities.
- Inflation makes a huge difference. Neglecting to take inflation into account can severely hurt your chances of achieving your financial goals.
- If your current lifestyle doesn't match your income, you're going to want to change things up a bit. Your lifestyle should allow you to save money every month. If it doesn't, you may need to cut some costs or adjust your spending habits.

- It's important to hold yourself accountable for your spending habits. Having a sense of accountability will ultimately help you achieve your financial goals. Don't beat yourself up if you mess up, but do take responsibility for your actions.

SEGUE

Now that you've learned about the first action step (setting specific and effective financial goals), you can move on to step 2: getting a job. Getting a job can be difficult, especially for young adults who don't have any work experience. In the next chapter, I'll go over the ins and outs of job searching as a young person, so stick around!

3

ACTION STEP 2: EARN ACTIVE INCOME

The road to financial independence doesn't have to be long and grueling. Making good financial decisions while also generating an income for yourself is totally possible — even if you don't have any work experience under your belt. Even if you're still a student, the benefits of having a part-time job or some sort of side hustle are unlimited. Not only will working an entry-level, part-time job give you valuable work experience, but it will also allow you to save money while you're studying.

Most colleges offer a work-study program, which is a fantastic way for students to get experience in their field of choice. Some work-study positions (i.e. resident advisor) allow students to save money on things like food and housing, which means you'll be able to put money towards your future early if you secure one of these positions. If college isn't for you, don't worry. There are plenty of jobs available to those who are interested in joining the workforce straight out of high school!

Of course, there's a lot to learn when you get your first job, but that's what makes it so exciting. Consider this quote from Chitra Reddy on Wisestep: "What do people learn from their first job? Your first job can teach you many things but the most important thing your first job can teach you is communicating with others. The employee learns the way he needs to speak with other employees, managers, and bosses. Effective communication in a fast-paced environment is something an employee learns." Breaking into the workforce is all about getting a foot in the door. Once you get your foot in the door, you'll be that much closer to finding success.

It's important to keep in mind that your first job probably isn't going to be your dream job. When seeking out your first job, you need to be realistic about what you're capable of. There's no need to feel discouraged, though, because your first job is mainly a learning experience. You've got to think long-term and set down the building blocks that will be the foundation for your future career. These building blocks may shift or tumble from time to time, but that's okay. It's just part of the experience, and one of these days — once you've learned all there is to learn — you'll reach the top.

It's also worth mentioning that your first job may not be in a field you're particularly interested in, and that's okay too. When a friend of mine was in high school, she worked at McDonald's every summer for the sole purpose of saving money. By the time she went to college, she had a solid emergency fund set up and was able to spend her time volunteering at the clinical lab on campus. She got her foot in the door, and was eventually able to get a paying job at the clinical lab, which had been her main goal.

So, you see? No matter what your first job ends up being, it's a good idea to take your long-term goals into consideration. My friend wasn't working at McDonald's in high school because she had dreams of being a manager there (though, there's of course nothing wrong with that). She was simply saving up money so that she could do what she loved — and make money doing what she loved — later on. I'm not trying to say that this process always goes smoothly for everyone who tries it. Life is complicated. My friend didn't find success without having to deal with some major setbacks along the way.

Figuring out your career isn't going to be a walk in the park, but the good news is, you just have to take it one day at a time. Start by getting your first job, and go from there. The most important thing for you right now, as a young person, is to earn some sort of active income. That way, you'll have the opportunity to start saving early. Let's go over what it means to earn active income in a bit more detail below.

WHAT IS ACTIVE INCOME?

For your first job, you'll most likely be earning an active income. To put it simply, active income is the money you earn actively working. You're providing your employer with your time and effort, and in exchange for that, you get paid. If you get paid a salary or make an hourly wage, let's say, working at a restaurant or in a retail environment, that's an example of active income. Furthermore, if you run your own business or do free-lance work, you'll also be earning an active income. Basically, you have to put in effort to earn this type of income. If you earn money without putting in any direct and constant effort (i.e. collecting rental income if you run an Airbnb, or gaining royalties from intellectual property) you're earning a passive income.

It's important to note that active income includes wages, your salary, net earnings from self-employment, and commissions — as well as any tips or bonuses you earn while working. There are a number of requirements a business owner must satisfy if they want income for their employees to be considered active instead of passive. These requirements are generally based on the number of hours employees work, and whether or not that work meets the Internal Revenue Service (IRS) definition of material participation.

With active income, there will always be a steady flow of money going into your savings account, just as long as you're actually working. If you work at a restaurant and receive a paycheck every two weeks (and tips every night), for example, you're an active income earner! Earning an active income is an excellent way for young people to save money because it provides workers with a significant amount of earnings fairly often. For this reason, seeking out a job where you earn active income is a great way to make and save money relatively quickly.

Let's look at some more examples of jobs that provide active income, just so you know exactly what to seek out while job-hunting. For instance, suppose two college students — Alyssa and Tyler — are studying at the same university. While Alyssa comes from a wealthy family, Tyler has to rely on a scholarship and student loans to pay for school. Tyler, therefore, decides to get a part-time job at Pizza Hut so that he can afford rent while studying. Alyssa, on the other hand, decides to invest her money in some stocks (because she has money to spare).

In this example, Tyler is earning an active income while Alyssa is earning a passive income. Both were able to save money, but the ways in which they decided to *make* money differed based on their life circumstances. Because Alyssa didn't have to worry much about making money, she was able to take her time and invest in stocks. Tyler, however, needed to make money fairly quickly so that he could afford rent while also saving up for his future and investing in his education. Does that make sense?

Let's take a look at another scenario. Two brothers, Max and Aaron, have just graduated from high school and are trying to decide what they want to do with their summer vacation. Max knows the owner of a local coffee shop in town and is able to secure a part-time job there. He earns a paycheck every two weeks and takes home tips after every shift. Max, therefore, is earning an active income. Aaron, however, has trouble finding a day job and instead decides to sell his photography online. He realizes this is risky, and that he won't be making a guaranteed income like his brother, but it's a good side hustle for the time being. Aaron, in this example, would be earning a passive income, assuming his photography actually sells.

Both of these scenarios demonstrate that working a job with an active income is typically much more stable than investing in stocks or attempting to sell your intellectual property for passive income. There's nothing wrong with earning a passive income, but you've got to keep in mind that this method of making money comes with a fair amount of uncertainty. For this reason, it's recommended that young people earn an active income *before* they try to earn a passive income. That's the other thing: plenty of people do both, and you can too! I just recommend you take it slow and steady.

WHY IT'S IMPORTANT TO GET A JOB AT A YOUNG AGE

The part-time summer job was an absolute staple for most high school students back when things were a little simpler, but since the intensity of the college application process started ramping up, the number of teens in the workforce has dropped significantly. Most high school seniors these days are taking on unpaid internships and volunteer positions the summer before they start college in order to plump up their resumes and college applications. This isn't necessarily a bad thing, and working as an unpaid intern *can* help you get a foot in the door, but you're not going to be making any money in the meantime.

Some high school students feel like they can do it all — the internship, the volunteer work, the part-time job — but these students generally have to give up any semblance of a work-life balance just to make ends meet. Saving money and plumping up your college applications are both important, but what happens when you get burnt out from working too much? What happens when college starts up in the fall? You'll be too tired to even get excited about starting what should be an especially formidable part of your life.

A big part of the problem is that the college application process has become too intense for a lot of people, especially those who wish to attend 4-year universities. On top of having a jam-packed resume and a brilliant grade point average, you have to score exceptionally well on the SAT test and then pour your heart out in your college admissions essay — and that's just what it takes to get *into* college. Furthermore, students who are struggling financially typically have to spend their summers applying for scholarships, which is both time-consuming and labor-intensive. Because of this, a lot of high school students don't have time to work summer jobs. Not these days, at least.

Now, before we dive into the importance of getting a job at a young age, I feel it's worth mentioning that attending a community college for two years and then finishing up at a 4-year university could be financially beneficial for, well, *anyone* who wants to pursue higher education. Going this particular route would also allow you to work more hours the summer before college starts, meaning you'd be able to save up plenty of money for school, rent, other expenses, and your future.

With that said, let's get into how and why having a part-time job as a young person could help you set up a foundation for future success.

You'll Learn Responsibility

If you're the oldest sibling in your household, you probably already know a thing or two about responsibility! Perhaps you had to watch your younger siblings while your parents were busy working, or maybe you took care of the family dog while everyone else was out of town. Homework teaches teens responsibility as well. At that age, your responsibility is to do your homework, and failing to do so has consequences — just like when you don't show up for work as an adult!

All adults have a sense of responsibility, even if that responsibility isn't necessarily work-related. You have a responsibility to pay your rent and feed your cat. You're responsible for paying your taxes and getting the oil changed in your car — you know, all of that fun stuff. Teenagers and young adults who have part-time jobs are likely to learn responsibility at a faster pace. By getting a part-time job when you're still young, you're essentially training yourself to be a responsible adult later in life.

You'll Gain an Understanding of the Value of Money

When you were a young teenager, you probably asked your parents for money at least once. Most teens do, and it's nothing to be ashamed of. Your parents want to support you the best they can, and most agree that it's okay to ask for money if you promise to pay it back eventually (which is why you probably shouldn't ask your parents for huge amounts of money). Asking your parents for money isn't very sustainable anyway, which is why it's so important for you to understand the value of money.

Teens and young adults who get part-time jobs have the opportunity to learn that money is something that's hard-earned. When you get your first job, you'll finally understand why your dad always said things like "I'm not made of money, you know" and "how did I become your personal ATM?" while you were growing up. You'll also learn how to properly manage your money, meaning you'll be able to invest in your future.

You'll Gain Work Experience

One of the main issues young adults run into when their job-hunting is their lack of work experience. A lot of young adults don't start working until after they graduate from college. However, many find it difficult to find a job due to their lack of experience, even if they have a Bachelor's degree. Filling up your resume with part-time jobs as a teenager is an excellent way to secure a job for yourself as an adult. Employers are much more likely to pick someone experienced over someone who's inexperienced, so I suggest becoming a jack of all trades while you're still young.

Now, admittedly, getting your first job without any experience whatsoever can be tricky. Not everyone is willing to hire teenagers, especially for jobs that pay decently well. When job-hunting as a teen, it's a good idea to look for jobs that advertise things like "willing to train" and "no experience necessary." Oftentimes, restaurants and retail stores are just looking for people who are willing to work. Show an employer that you're a good worker, and you should have no problem getting your first job. It also helps to have connections, so if you happen to know people, you should definitely use that to your advantage!

You'll Get to Know the Real World

I learned more about people working at a fast food restaurant after college than I did in any college psychology class. College is wonderful, but it's often a bubble. If you don't work while in college, you're essentially closing yourself off from the real world — which can frankly be quite frightening and harsh. If you get a job as a high school or college student, however, you'll get exposure to the bitterness of the real world. What's more, you'll learn to accept it. There will be difficult days for sure, but in the end, you'll grow a thicker skin and perhaps even laugh at the absurdity of it all.

It's also important to keep in mind that restaurant and retail jobs are temporary for most people. There are absolutely people who do it for their whole lives, but the people I've known who are in those positions tend to love it despite the fact it's hard. If you don't love it, that's totally okay and you'll eventually find something new. You've got to keep things in perspective and find the humor in the strange and often rude things customers say and do. That's what helped me get through that stage in my life.

You'll Become Financially Independent

Everyone loves payday. There are few things more satisfying than getting paid for all of the hard work you've been doing. Not only is it emotionally rewarding, but you'll also have your very own money to spend and save (emphasis on "save"). Having a source of income will also help you develop a sense of independence. You won't have to ask your parents for money or rely on birthday cash from your grandmother anymore. You'll be able to pay for your own food and clothes, as well as save up money for college and a car.

Just make sure to apply your sense of responsibility when you become financially independent. Too many young people spend too much money on things they don't really need directly after getting paid. I'm guilty of it, myself: "I just got paid, so it's fine if I splurge on this fancy meal or a new pair of shoes." A lot of people who are new to being financially independent will adopt an "I'll make it back" mindset, which is a dangerous road to go down. Be happy that you're finally financially independent, but take it easy on the spending, and don't forget to set some money aside for savings. You'll certainly thank yourself for it later.

HOW TO FIND A JOB WHEN YOU HAVE LITTLE TO NO EXPERIENCE

Job-hunting can be frustrating, especially if you don't have any work experience under your belt. Perhaps you've been in this position before. You need work experience in order to get a job, but you need a job in order to get work experience. When you explain this to employers, they typically give you a sympathetic look and say: "sorry, kid, but so-and-so is a better candidate because they have experience." It can truly feel like a never-ending cycle.

Thankfully, there are a few strategies you can use to make landing your first job just a little bit easier. Keep in mind that you might strike out a couple of times before you succeed, but it's important not to get discouraged. Keep trying, and keep applying. It may take some time, but you'll get there!

Write and Format Your Resume

I'm not going to sugar-coat this. Writing a good resume is honestly quite difficult — especially if you don't have any previous work experience. It's not something you're born knowing how to do, and oftentimes, you have to halfway guess at what specific employers actually want to see on a resume. For this reason, it's a good idea to apply for jobs that specify what sort of employee is wanted in the job description. Consider what skills the company you're interested in working for is seeking out, and outline your resume based on these skills.

In general, your resume should show that you're adaptable, commercially aware, and a great team player. Most employers want to be sure that you're going to make their company money, and that you're going to stick around for a while. This doesn't mean you have to sign your life away. It just means you have to *say* you'll be around for a while. While this is technically dishonest, you can't know for sure how long you'll be at a specific job, *especially* if it's your first job. Do what you have to do to get the job in the first place, *then* decide what you want to do from there.

In terms of formatting, most employers won't expect an entry-level resume to look perfect. In general, though, your resume should start with your education followed by your work experience, your volunteer work, and your hobbies. Keep in mind that most employers will only skim your resume, so keep it concise and be sure to include plenty of buzzwords. You want your resume to look clean and professional, but content is definitely key.

Explain Your Lack of Work Experience

When explaining your lack of work experience to employers, it's important that you avoid being overly apologetic. Apologizing too much shows a lack of confidence, and most employers don't want to hear a bunch of "I'm sorries" anyway. It's important to be honest about your lack of experience when applying for jobs, but don't place so much emphasis on your lack of experience that it's all potential employers are able to see.

Tell employers: "while I have a lack of work experience due to the fact I'm only in high school, I have plenty to offer to your company." From there, you can list your skills and direct the employer's attention *away* from your lack of experience. Show them that you are committed to the role you're applying for. Employers want to see drive and determination from employees, so be confident! Personality and posture can make a big difference, so practice in the mirror and don't forget to smile during your interview.

Stand Out to Employers

While lots and lots of experience looks great on a resume, it's not the only thing employers are looking for when assessing whether or not someone will be a good fit for an open position at their company. Your employer will want to see evidence that you'll be able to build strong relationships with your coworkers and clients, and that you'll perform well under pressure. They may ask you to discuss a time when you had to overcome a particular challenge or conflict. Being able to answer this question without hesitation will show that you're prepared and well-organized, which will also look good to employers.

If you don't have a lot of work experience, you'll need to consider the challenges you've faced while participating in extra-curricular activities. These activities may include sporting events, and side gigs like babysitting and dog walking. You can also talk about the role you've played in group projects for school, or discuss a situation in which you facilitated a conversation between two friends who were having a disagreement. Be creative, be confident, and *prepare* if you want to stand out to employers.

INTERACTIVE ELEMENT

Write down any action steps you'd like to take in regard to what you've learned in this chapter. These can be bullet points, and they don't have to be set in stone. Just think of this as a space to brainstorm your ideas!

SEGUE

Once you get a job, you'll need to learn how to be responsible with your earnings. In the next chapter, I'll discuss the actions you need to take if you want to properly manage your money. I'll also go over how to get out of debt, as well as dive into how to avoid getting into debt in the first place.

4

ACTION STEP 3: BE DISCIPLINED WITH YOUR MONEY

M anaging your money can be challenging, especially for those of us who aren't particularly mathematically inclined. Proper money management, as I stated before, isn't something you learn in high school. Most people have to learn about proper money management the hard way. For example, my parents recently paid off a ton of credit card debt that had accumulated over several years — the result of their being irresponsible with their money when they were in their early thirties. They had bad credit for quite a while because of this, and being neck-deep in debt meant they had to pinch pennies just to make ends meet.

Life can be expensive. This is especially true now with inflation on the rise. It's no surprise that most young people are spending more than they can afford. To make matters worse, the majority of young people never learned how to budget properly. Many are already in debt due to an accumulation of student loans. Clearly, as a young person, it's very easy to find yourself in a whole lot of debt fairly quickly. For this reason, it's a good idea to learn how to manage your money efficiently from the start — ideally *before* you get yourself into a mountain of debt.

Consider this quote from Latitude: "Being financially responsible means living within your means. It really is that simple – and a budget is the crucial first step. Keeping track of your income and expenses may help you spend less than you earn. You can also factor in saving, or paying off any existing debt." When budgeting, you've got to take your earnings into consideration. If you spend more than you earn every month, you're probably going to get yourself into financial trouble.

Building up a healthy savings account will also significantly benefit you. Not only will it give you financial security, but it will give you peace of mind as well. Emergencies happen, and when they do happen, you want to be prepared. A lot of young adults will decide to get a credit card "for emergencies only," but this is actually a terrible idea. Budgeting, in this particular case, is actually quite multi-layered. You should budget your earnings as a whole, but you should also budget your savings (i.e. set a certain amount of savings aside for emergencies).

Basically, you should have emergency savings (which you're allowed to touch but *for emergencies only*), and future savings (which you're not allowed to touch *at all*). That way, you'll have money in your savings account no matter what. A big part of being an adult is learning how to be disciplined with yourself. While treating yourself once in a while is important, the "treat yourself" mentality has gotten a little bit out of control as of late.

When I was in college, my friends and I would frequently order pizza or Doordash because "we needed food to help us study" and "didn't have time to cook." Obviously, this kind of lifestyle wasn't sustainable. I didn't even realize how much money I was spending per month until I actually went over my bank statements. When I saw the amount of money I was spending on food delivery, my heart dropped into my stomach. I realized, right then and there, that I seriously had to reevaluate my spending habits.

Way too many young people find themselves in this same situation for a variety of reasons. A lot of college students partake in alcohol and marijuana consumption, which can significantly impair your judgment and decision-making skills. A friend of mine, who worked for a food delivery service for a couple of years, once asked me to guess who the majority of his customers were. "Drunk people?" I guessed, and he smiled sheepishly. "Yep. And young stoners. They answer the door, and are clearly intoxicated. But, hey. Intoxicated people tip well."

This is another reason why it's a good idea to build yourself a healthy savings account. If you've promised yourself that you can't touch the money in your savings account, then you can't touch the money in your savings account. Period. If you don't have enough personal spending money to order pizza when you're hungry, pick yourself up and walk or drive to the nearest convenience store. You'd be surprised what you can do with a pack of instant ramen and whatever you happen to have in your fridge. It may not be ideal, but you'll thank yourself for sticking to your budget.

WHY YOU NEED TO LEARN HOW TO MANAGE YOUR EARNINGS

There are a number of reasons why learning how to properly manage your earnings is absolutely crucial. It's common for young people (but not just young people!) to spend a significant amount of their biweekly paycheck on unnecessary expenses. When you factor in the cost of living, gas, food, and bills, it's no surprise that so many people are living paycheck to paycheck. If you start budgeting and saving, however, you might find that you don't actually have to live this way. Listed below are some reasons why you need to learn how to manage your earnings:

You'll Save For Your Future

When you get your paycheck each week (or every other week), it's very important that you set some of that money aside for savings. Admittedly, when you're holding your hard-earned money in your hand, it can be tempting to spend it on something you've been wanting for a while — like a shopping spree or a new video game. However, it makes more sense in the long run to set that money aside until you can make those purchases without wreaking havoc on your conscience.

Initially, it may be hard to gauge how much money you should put into your savings account every week. This is why it's a good idea to budget. Sit down and take the time to really figure out your weekly expenses. It's also a good idea to start small if you're new to the concept of saving money. Try putting $50 into your savings account after each pay period, and increase the amount from there if it feels manageable.

You'll Get Great at Budgeting

Learning how to budget your money isn't as scary as it sounds. The first thing you're going to want to do when creating a budget for yourself is to consider how much you earn each week — as well as how much you spend each week. Creating a weekly budget might initially be easier than creating a monthly budget, but it depends on a variety of factors. Follow your gut and do what will work best for you!

Let's say you work at a restaurant or retail store, and bring home about $400 a week. I recommend writing down all of the things you typically spend money on in a week, just so you can easily keep track of your spending. Let's say your share of the rent and bills typically comes out to $500 a month. Since you're making $400 a week, you can set aside $125 each week for rent and bills. From there, you can set aside $40 for things like food and coffee, $20 for gas or public transportation fees, and $15 for a special treat. You're left with $200 now, which means you can put $100 into your savings account and use the rest as spending or emergency money.

See what I mean? When you lay it all out on the table, it doesn't seem so complicated. You'll have to tailor your budget depending on how much you earn — which may involve some trial and error — but you'll eventually figure out a budget plan that best suits your needs and spending habits.

You'll Develop Important Life and Work Skills

Learning how to manage your money won't just benefit you financially. It will also help you develop useful life and work skills, such as discipline, organization, initiative, and negotiation. By putting away a small amount of your earnings each week, you'll be disciplining yourself. This sense of discipline will in turn enhance your decision-making skills because you'll have to think very carefully about your spending habits. Budgeting is also a fantastic way to practice your organizational skills. You'll know exactly where all of your money is going each week, and that will give you peace of mind.

Managing your earnings can also help you develop your employability skills, which will help you get more jobs in the future. By taking control of your money, you're taking initiative, which will show potential employers that you'll be an excellent addition to their company. When budgeting, you'll likely be shopping around for the best money-saving methods, which is a great way to develop your negotiation skills.

DEBT: HOW TO GET OUT AND STAY OUT OF IT

It's difficult to go through life without getting into some sort of debt at some point. For many young people, the first debt they'll find themselves in takes the form of student loans. Most would agree that higher education is overly expensive in the United States. Tuition at Ivy League schools in particular honestly verges on predatory. It discourages poor students from applying, which means these students might not be able to reach their full potential. For this reason, many students end up taking out a frightening amount of loans to be able to afford school. The problem is, the average student won't be able to afford to pay back these loans within their lifetime.

Thankfully, though, getting out of debt is completely possible if you're willing to put the time and effort in. It's like digging yourself out of a hole. I can't promise you that it's going to be easy, but you *will* get out of this. Assessing the damage report is the first step to getting out of debt. Debt is a common problem, and if you're like most people, you may have a lot of it. Take a deep breath, and initiate the damage control. The longer you wait to address this issue, the more debt you're likely to accumulate.

Listed below are several strategies you can use to dig yourself out of debt. Keep in mind that getting out of debt is a long process, and you may run into some occasional setbacks. As you start this process, keep these strategies up your sleeve. You'll find that managing your debt — and staying out of it for good — is totally in the cards for you.

Evaluate Your Past Debt

If you're going to dig yourself out of your debt, you should first try to gain an understanding of where you went wrong in the first place. Consider your past spending habits. Were you attempting to live beyond your means? Did you use your credit card for unnecessary expenses or take out student loans to make your education more affordable? If so, you're definitely not alone. These things happen, but understanding how and why they happened to you can help you avoid similar missteps.

Build an Emergency Fund

Creating and building an emergency fund is honestly one of the best things you can do for yourself. You never know when you're going to have to rush to the emergency room or get work done on your car after an accident has occurred. Start out by putting $50 into your savings account every week. After a while, your account will grow and you'll be covered when it comes to emergency expenses. Needless to say, it can be kind of a bummer to have to dip into your savings, but think of it this way: the money you're saving is specifically for emergencies, and in the long run, you'll be saving yourself from credit card debt.

Budget Wisely and Spend Only What You Have

Once you get a solid grasp on your finances, you should be able to avoid taking out loans. Take your spending habits into consideration, and create a budget for yourself. Separate your expenses into "mandatory" and "not mandatory." Consider whether you really *need* to be going out for dinner every week, or whether buying that new pair of shoes over the weekend was necessary. Budgeting is a great way to ensure that you have money left over at the end of each week to put into your savings account, meaning you'll have an easier time staying out of debt in the long run. Something I started doing a long time ago was moving money over into my savings account when I was about to buy a new pair of shoes that I didn't need. I wasn't going to miss the money anyway so I just move that $100 over.

Find a Side Gig

There's nothing wrong with having a side hustle or two! As you're probably well aware, the cost of living is on the rise, which means most Americans need to supplement their income somehow. It's generally quite easy to find a side gig if you know where to look. A friend of mine was able to make over $5,000 last year walking dogs and pet sitting through an app. This gave her more room to breathe financially, and she got to put some extra spending money in her wallet as well. It's definitely worth it!

Cut Unnecessary Expenses

Most people aren't even aware of how much money they're spending per month on things like gym memberships and streaming subscriptions. These things add up, and can end up ruining your ability to budget successfully. Consider how often you actually use streaming subscriptions. Cancel your gym membership, and start going for runs outside. You might find that you enjoy that even more than jogging on a treadmill once every few weeks! I'm not saying you have to cut everything, but cutting the monthly subscriptions that you're not really using can help you save a surprising amount of money after all is said and done.

Take Advantage of Automation

Budgeting manually can be a pain, and as human beings, we're prone to making mistakes that could potentially be costly. Consider using an automation app to help you budget accurately and avoid late fees. It can be difficult to keep track of things like rent, bills, and credit card payments, but if you set up automated payments you won't have to worry about it so much.

Nip Potential Debt in the Bud

If you do find yourself needing to borrow money (it happens), you can save yourself a lot of trouble by nipping it in the bud as soon as possible. Figure out which of your debts comes with the highest interest rate (for most, this is credit card debt). Prioritize paying off this debt first as it's probably what's going to cause you the most trouble. Don't wait to pay off debts either, as late fees will only give you more financial hardship.

AN INTRODUCTION TO BUDGETING

What is budgeting, exactly? To put things plainly, budgeting is essentially the process you go through when you come up with a plan to spend (or save) your earnings. The great thing about creating a budget is that it will allow you to know in advance how much money you'll be able to spend in different areas of your life for a given amount of time. When following a set budget, you'll be able to prioritize what's most important — such as rent, bills, food, savings, and emergency money.

Why is Budgeting so Important?

Once you learn how to create a good budget for yourself, and — even more importantly — learn how to successfully stick to that budget, you'll understand why budgeting is necessary. Budgeting ensures that you'll always have enough money on hand, which means you won't have to use your credit card for emergency situations and unnecessary spending. It can help you avoid falling into a pit of debt, as well as give you peace of mind that you'll be able to pay for your mandatory expenses each month.

What About Budget Forecasting and Planning?

It's generally a good idea to map out your expenses for at least six months to a year when creating a budget plan. Doing this will give you the ability to forecast which months your finances might be a little tighter than usual. For most people, the winter months can be a bit more expensive because heating bills tend to be higher. During these months, you should try to save more and spend less on non-necessities than your regular budget allows. Also, when you extend your budget into the future, you'll be able to determine how much money you'll need to save for things like rainy days, vacations, and special dinners down the line.

HOW TO CREATE A BUDGET AND STICK TO IT

Effective budgeting takes practice. As I said before, you might go through a period of trial and error, and that's okay! The first step to creating a budget for yourself involves getting a full picture of how much you earn and how much you typically spend within a certain amount of time. Once you've got that information laid out in front of you, you should be able to determine how much you spend on non-necessities and set aside that money for savings or an emergency fund instead.

One of the hardest parts of creating a budget is sticking to it after the fact. You might be tempted to dip into your savings, say, if your friends invite you out for dinner, or if you see something at the store that you just *have* to have. The great thing about budgeting is, if you're able to save enough over time, you'll be able to treat yourself to things like this once in a while. It might not be easy at first, but once you get into the swing of things, you'll find that all of that time and effort you put into budgeting and saving was worth it.

It's important to keep in mind that your spending habits won't necessarily change overnight. If you're going to stick to your budget, there are a few tips you'll want to take into consideration. First of all, you should hold yourself accountable. Promise yourself that you're going to stick to your budget no matter what. Be realistic and keep a close eye on your finances every week. You may find it helpful to keep track of your spending in a small journal. That way, you can determine where you're spending too much and tweak your budget and spending habits as needed.

It's also a good idea to set goals for yourself. You're much more likely to stick to your budget and save money if you have something you're specifically working towards. When you complete one of your goals, reward yourself in some small way. Again, I recommend keeping track of your goals in a journal or spreadsheet as that will help you stay up to date on your progress. If you find yourself struggling to stick to your budget, don't be afraid to seek out moral support from your friends or family members. It can't hurt to have a strong support system in place!

As an example, I've included my personal budgeting breakdown below. You can use this as a template for your own budgeting plan if you wish to. Just remember to create your budget based on your own earnings and lifestyle.

MY PERSONAL BUDGETING BREAKDOWN

- 55% - Essentials (Food, Gas, Bills)
- 10% - Long-Term Saving (Rainy Day Fund, Vacations, etc)
- 10% - Education (Mentorship, Books, etc.)
- 10% - Financial Freedom Account (Investments, Retirement, etc)
- 5-10% - Giving (Charities, Church, etc)
- 5-10% - Play Money (SPEND ON YOURSELF)

THE STORY OF BOB AND SUZIE

If you're currently in debt, just know that I've been there too. I know it's not easy to live within your means, especially when you're young and have a mountain of debt looming over you. There are plenty of success stories out there, though, and you can be one of them if you're willing to take back control of your life. Take the story of Bob and Suzie, who were struggling to make ends meet due to childcare expenses, buying a home, and using credit to buy furniture and appliances.

Bob and Suzie simply wanted to do what was best for their family, and they felt like they had no other choice but to rely on credit for things like upgrading their cars and dealing with financial shortfalls. After a certain point, they became worried that they would have to sell their home or declare bankruptcy. They simply owed too much money for their level of income. Not knowing what else to do, they met with a credit counselor, who helped them review their options.

She helped them figure out the amount of equity they had built up on their house, which ended up being enough to pay off their car loans. Once they got that sorted, they were able to start making debt repayments. The credit counselor even helped them enroll in a debt management program, which consolidated all of their loans and made the amount they owed easier to keep track of.

With Bob and Suzie's debt getting smaller over time, they were able to start building an emergency fund for their family, an education fund for their kids, and a retirement fund for themselves. Eventually, they were able to pay off all of their accumulated debt, and they didn't even have to empty their bank account to do so.

So, you see? Even if you're neck-deep in debt, getting back on track is absolutely possible if you're willing to do what it takes to help yourself.

INTERACTIVE ELEMENT

Want to take a short quiz to test your knowledge? Let's see what you've learned!

1. What should you do if you want to stay out of debt? (Select all that apply)

    a. Build an emergency fund.
    b. Find a side gig.
    c. Cut unnecessary expenses.
    d. Ask your parents for money.

2. Why is it important to learn how to manage your earnings? (Select all that apply)

    a. You'll become better at budgeting.
    b. You'll develop important life skills.
    c. You'll spend less on non-necessities.
    d. You'll be able to save more money.

3. Why is budgeting so important? (Select all that apply)

    a. It ensures that you'll always have money available.
    b. It can help you avoid debt.
    c. Budgeting is not that important.
    d. If you budget, you'll be able to eat out more often.

4. What is true about budgeting? (Select all that apply)

    a. Budgeting can help you save money.
    b. If you budget, you won't be able to do fun things ever again.
    c. Budgeting can help you build an emergency fund.
    d. Budgeting can give you peace of mind about your finances.

Answer Key:

1. a), b), and c)
2. All of the above
3. a) and b)
4. a), c), and d)

SEGUE

Now that you've learned about budgeting, it's time to start thinking about how you're going to save up your money. In the next chapter, I'll go over the best ways to start saving your earnings (spoiler alert: it's not *just* about pinching pennies).

5

ACTION STEP 4: SAVE UP

W hat are some of your main goals in life? Perhaps you dream of traveling the world someday, or maybe you want to fall in love, settle down, and have a family. Perhaps you want to travel the world *with* your family, or maybe — for now — you just want to be able to pay rent at your apartment without having to scrimp and pinch pennies each month. Needless to say, it's going to be easier for you to achieve your life goals if you have money saved up, but saving money isn't always that simple.

Or is it? Admittedly, there's a difference between "simple" and "easy," but if you're able to form a saving habit rather than a spending habit, you'll find that saving up your money isn't so difficult after all. Take this quote from Finance Over Fifty: "There are many reasons you may be challenged to save money. Some of those could include a high cost of living, too much debt, overspending, lifestyle inflation, or lack of a budget. Saving money is a habit that can typically be developed by taking simple steps to cut expenses and increase income."

Now, I'm not saying saving money is a walk in the park. For most people, saving money takes exceptional restraint and strict budgeting — especially at first. Saving money also requires some sacrifice. Let's say, for example, your friend makes six figures and is able to afford to go out to brunch every weekend. She invites you out with her, and despite the fact she makes a lot more money than you do, she insists on splitting the bill. This feels technically fair (if a bit selfish), and you don't want to miss out on a delicious brunch with your friend, so you say to yourself: "Hey, it's fine. I'll make that money back."

The problem is, by going out to brunch every weekend, you're attempting to live beyond your means. In other words, it's not sustainable. If you find yourself dipping into your savings once a week for brunch with your rich friend, you're not actually going to be able to save all that much money in the long run. You've got to think about how much money you'll be saving each week by sacrificing your brunch craving. If brunch costs $75 (not including the tip), and you're going out every weekend, then that's at least $300 *per month* that could have gone to your emergency or retirement fund. The fear of missing out is very real — trust me, I get it — but by giving into your FOMO, you're financially shooting yourself in the foot. This is a sacrifice that is absolutely worth making. Also, it might be time to distance yourself from that particular friend, anyway.

What most people don't realize is, saving money takes more than just putting a portion of your paycheck into your savings account every two weeks. You've got to plan, strategize, and effectively budget — otherwise you're going to have no choice but to dip into your savings for necessities like food and rent money. Way too many young people just sort of "wing it" when it comes to saving money. They never learned how to budget and save, and for most it feels too early to start thinking about things like marriage and retirement.

The fact of the matter is, you're going to benefit significantly if you start saving up your money at an early age. Oftentimes, the older you get, the more expensive life tends to become. When you move out of your parents' house, you suddenly have rent and utility bills to worry about. If you save up and buy yourself a car, you've got to remember to put money aside for your monthly insurance payments. Depending on the type of lifestyle you want to live, keeping track of your finances as an adult can honestly be quite complicated.

For this reason, it's a good idea to get into the habit of saving your money and tracking your spending habits while you're still young. It may seem like somewhat of a drag at first, but again, you've got to think about the long-term. Traveling the world, getting married, and having kids are all wonderful goals, but they're very expensive. If you start saving your money now, you'll be able to avoid a major financial headache (and live your best life) in the long run.

HOW YOU CAN BENEFIT FROM STARTING TO SAVE UP MONEY AT AN EARLY AGE

Our habits have a lot of power over us, don't they? When you develop a habit, it becomes engrained in your brain — much like when an indentation forms along the path you always walk. This is why it's a good idea to start putting your money away now. Eventually, saving money will become a habit for you, just as much as spending money might be a habit for you in this current moment.

Once you start gathering money over time, you'll feel more inclined to continue to save it. If you have or have ever had a nest egg (in other words, a sum of money saved up for your future), you know how relieving and rewarding saving money can be. You also probably know how difficult it can be. For most people, making money is honestly really hard. It's even more challenging to make "enough" money to survive, especially with inflation and the fluctuating economy throwing a wrench into people's financial plans.

As I said before, life is only going to become more complicated and expensive as you get older. You'll find that each day is unpredictable, and that jobs are fairly easy to lose (if the company you're working for has to downsize, for example). This lack of stability can make getting older a bit of a financial shock to the system for young people who simply weren't prepared by their parents or their education system to understand the financial burdens that come with adulthood.

As you enter into adulthood, it's important that you don't let life pull the rug out from under your feet. Don't wait to start working towards your financial goals, and put away as much money for the future as you're able to. You'll see, in time, just how much saving your money at a young age can benefit you. Let's go over the various benefits in a bit more detail below so you can get the full picture:

Think About Your Retirement

You might feel like you're too young to start thinking about your retirement, but that is very much not the case. It's never too early to start saving up for your retirement, even if you don't have a stable job and income yet. If you haven't already, go to the bank and open up a savings account. Most people don't start saving for retirement until they're well into their twenties, but honestly, the sooner you're able to start saving, the better. Did you get some birthday or graduation cash from a friend or family member recently? Instead of spending it on a snazzy pair of shoes, put it into your savings account! Even if it's only $20, you've got to start somewhere.

Time is on Your Side

The great thing about starting a savings account while you're still young is that you'll have plenty of *time* to save up plenty of money. Think about it. If you were to start saving up for your retirement in your forties, you wouldn't be able to build a very big retirement package for yourself overall. If you start saving up in your twenties, however, your retirement package could end up being twice as big. So, if you're young and worried about money, take a breath. As long as you start saving now, you'll have time to dig yourself out of debt as well as save for your future.

Learn from Your Successes (and Failures)

When saving up money and learning how to budget as a young person, you're probably going to make a few mistakes along the way. This isn't anything you should fret about, though, because you can honestly learn a lot from your financial mistakes. Back in college, a friend of mine ended up buying a new computer after he got paid. Granted, his computer was so old that he couldn't run newer video games on it, and video games brought him a considerable amount of joy. The problem was, he wasn't actually able to afford a new computer. He ended up having to sell his new computer to be able to pay his rent.

Years later, he's still kicking himself because of that mistake. He had to work really hard to save up for *another* new computer while also saving up enough to pay for rent, utilities, and food. This was a simple but devastating budgeting mistake, meaning it probably never would have happened if my friend had had a solid budgeting plan in place at the time. He learned a lot about budgeting and being more financially responsible because of his mistake, though, so it might be for the best that it happened. Sometimes, you just have to learn these things the hard way. Alternatively, you could learn how to budget and save *before* you get yourself into financial trouble.

Don't Procrastinate

Did you ever wait until the last minute to complete an assignment when you were in high school or college? I know I did. The main reason teachers and professors give students future deadlines for their assignments is that learning how to manage your time appropriately and not procrastinate is a crucial life skill. Much like with an important homework assignment, you should avoid procrastinating at all costs (no pun intended) when it comes to saving money. Start saving now, and be disciplined. Don't give into peer pressure when your friends invite you out for a night on the town, especially if they invite you out for a night on the town *every weekend*. It'll take some restraint and adjustment for sure, but you can do it. I believe in you.

Save Efficiently and Waste Less Money

Saving money for your future (and your retirement) is a major commitment. As far as commitments go, this one is particularly easy to break. Some young people feel like they can't control their bad spending habits. They've grown accustomed to a certain lifestyle and their friends aren't financially responsible, so why should they have to be? There are plenty of problems with this mindset, but the main one is this: Being financially irresponsible when you're young is eventually going to come back and bite you. However, if you set up a budget and refuse to touch your savings account, you'll feel much more in control of your finances. You'll be able to save for your future and waste less money on unnecessary expenses.

THE BEST WAYS TO SAVE MONEY

Saving money can be tricky, but there are a number of strategies you can use to make forming a healthy saving habit just a little bit easier. Keep in mind that you're probably going to have to adjust your lifestyle, your spending habits, and the way you think about money in general if you want to be a successful saver. In this section, I'll go over some of the best money-saving methods I've come across throughout my life and my research. You can try each method or pick and choose the methods you think will work best for you. Either way, if you know you have trouble saving money, trying one or two of these strategies can't hurt!

General Savings Tips:

Set up an Emergency Fund

It probably seems like I'm trying to drill this advice into your head, but it's for a good reason. Emergencies happen, and they happen more often than you might think when you're an adult. You never know when you're going to get an outrageously expensive parking ticket, or a flat tire. If your pet gets sick and needs emergency surgery, you'll want to be absolutely sure that you can afford to pay for the veterinary bill. It's generally recommended that you build up an emergency fund that's equal to about three to six months of your income. This might seem like a lot, but you'll certainly be glad to have it when the time comes.

Establish Your Budget

If you're going to establish a good budget for yourself, the first thing you're going to want to do is maintain some semblance of organization regarding your spending habits. It's always a good idea to keep your receipts and separate them into categories — such as groceries, restaurants, healthcare, and pet supplies. This way, you'll be able to see exactly how much you spent on each category at the end of each month. Once you realize your spending habits, you'll be able to establish a budget and spend more wisely.

Save for Your Future

Remember, your future matters. If you save up money with your future in mind, you'll have a better incentive to continue to save and stick to your budget. Whether you're saving up for college, future travel expenses, retirement, or for emergencies, having a goal to look forward to while you're saving should help you stay inspired and motivated to keep at it.

Entertainment Savings Tips:

Check Out Your Local Library

Contrary to popular belief, there is such a thing as free entertainment. The last time I was visiting my hometown, I realized that I'd never actually been to the local library. I stopped by on a whim, and it turned out to be an absolute goldmine of free entertainment. While going to the library for fun might seem like something Willow Rosenberg or Velma Dinkley might do, those characters are great and so are libraries! You can borrow books, movies, and even sewing machines. Or, you can curl up in a comfy chair and read your favorite book series for hours.

Volunteer at Festivals

Going to a music festival or cultural festival is an incredible experience, but it's usually very expensive. Don't worry, though, because these types of festivals are always lacking in volunteers. Reach out to the people who are in charge of organizing your favorite festival or event and ask them if you can attend for free in exchange for helping out. I recommend asking them early, just in case there are a lot of people trying to volunteer. You might not be able to "let loose" as much as you'd like to if you're a volunteer at a festival, but hey, at least you'll get to *remember* the festival.

Attend Local Free or Low-Cost Events

Attending local events is an excellent way to have a great time in your community without spending a whole lot of money. You can usually find free or low-cost events on sites like Facebook and Eventbrite. You can also check out Groupon if you're looking to get a discount at your local movie theater or bowling alley. I actually had one of my most memorable experiences with my friends thanks to Groupon. It truly is an inexpensive, guilt-free way to have fun!

Family and Friends Savings Tips:

Discuss a Spending Limits on Gifts

There's nothing wrong with laying down the law and deciding to stick to a spending limit when it comes to holiday shopping for your friends and family members. Make a group chat with your loved ones and request that nobody spends more than $10 or $20 on one another (the actual amount will of course depend on what you can afford, budget-wise). Most of your friends and family members should be willing to abide by the spending limit, and it'll probably take some holiday stress off of their shoulders as well!

Plan Your Gift-Giving in Advance

The holidays tend to be a stressful (and expensive) time for most people. If you want to avoid stressing out over what you're going to get for your friends and family members, it's a good idea to plan it out ahead of time. Planning out your gifts for others in advance is also a great way to save money. More time means more wiggle room, so you won't have to settle on a gift card to your sister's favorite, super-expensive sushi restaurant just because you're out of other options as a result of procrastination.

Have One "No Spend Day" Per Week

It's always nice to spoil your loved ones, but there's no better gift for everyone involved than time well spent together. Try to designate at least one day a week as a "no spend day." Invite your friends over for dinner, and cook with whatever you happen to have in your fridge. Spend the evening playing board games or watching a movie that you already own. Everyone is sure to have a great time, and your friends will definitely thank you!

Food Savings Tips:

Eat Out Less

You've probably heard this one before, but it's true. Eating out less is going to help you save more money than you think it is. Trust me, I enjoy eating out just as much as anyone else, but it's no secret that going out for dinner is more expensive than cooking at home. I'm not saying you have to stop eating out entirely, but reducing the number of times you eat out per month could be extremely beneficial to your bank account.

Plan Your Meals in Advance

Have you ever gone grocery shopping while hungry and without a list? I have, and it wasn't pretty. I ended up spending way too much money on snacks and frozen food, which was bad for both my budget and my health. When grocery shopping, it's always a good idea to bring a list with you (and stick to it!) Planning out your meals in advance can help with this, as it'll motivate you to buy only what you need. I'm not saying you can't grab a special treat from the candy aisle once in a while, but it's best not to make a habit out of it.

Double Your Recipes

Doubling your recipes when you cook is a great way to get two meals out of one. My mother used to do this quite a lot. She'd make a boatload of spaghetti or meatloaf and we'd always have leftovers to eat the next day.

This is obviously an excellent way to save money, and it will save you a lot of cooking and kitchen clean-up work, too — which is always a plus.

Transportation Savings Tips:

Check Sites for the Lowest Airfares

Are you planning to take a trip anytime soon? Maybe it's been a while since you've spent time with your family, or perhaps you just need to get away for a bit. Whatever your reasons are for traveling, you should know that you don't have to break the bank just to get on a plane. Shop around on different sites for cheaper airline tickets, and pack efficiently so that you don't have to pay to check a lot of heavy luggage.

Take Public Transportation to Save on Gas

This advice is particularly helpful if you live in a big city. If you've ever driven in a city like Portland, OR, or San Francisco, CA, you know how much gas you waste just sitting in traffic for *hours*. While public transportation can occasionally be unreliable, it's usually a whole lot cheaper than driving. You also won't have to worry about finding and paying for parking when you take public transportation. That's a major stress reliever in my book!

BUILDING AN EMERGENCY FUND

Building an emergency fund is obviously necessary, but if you feel overwhelmed by the concept, that's totally understandable. The idea of saving up to three to six months of your income for emergency reasons might seem daunting, but it's possible if you're able to cut unnecessary costs and budget efficiently.

I also want to make this point — this is important to get done before you start investing. It pains me to say it but it's true and this strategy has helped me more than anything else in this book. If you are trying to invest all of your money first and neglecting your short-term emergency fund, it will come back to bite you at some point. Your investments are important but are pointless if life happens short-term and you do not have an emergency fund.

How does one begin to build an emergency fund? I'll break it down for you below so that you can take it one step at a time:

Step 1: Determine Your Monthly Expenses

When figuring out your monthly expenses, it might be helpful to write everything down in a notebook or journal. You've got to remember to factor in things like groceries, your phone bill, transportation, rent, utilities, your car insurance, and any money you typically have left over to spend on whatever you like. Add everything together and multiply that number by 3-6 months. That's the amount of money you'll need to have ready in an emergency savings account.

Step 2: Cut Costs

How much do you spend on coffee per month? How about things like pizza delivery, new clothes, and video games? These things are delightful, but they're often impulse purchases. Try giving up your daily to-go coffee for a week (you can always bring coffee from home), and put that money into your savings account instead. You might be surprised how much you're spending on things you don't really need.

Step 3: Automation is Your Friend

It's a good idea to treat your savings like any monthly bill. You wouldn't think twice about paying your car insurance or rent, so why would you neglect contributing to your savings account? I always try to put the amount I want to save into my savings account *on* payday, just so I don't get tempted. Your bank should be able to do this for you automatically, which should make things a bit easier.

Step 4: Start Small, then Build Up

When I was in my early twenties, I did a lot of gig work. This meant that I would get paid $400 or $500 at a time for specific jobs — which was lovely — but I wasn't making a consistent biweekly income and some jobs were few and far apart. I would usually get excited about suddenly having $500 dollars and decide to put $300 into my savings account without really thinking about all of my other expenses. I would always end up having to dip into my savings when it was time to pay rent, which was obviously kind of a bummer. I realized, at some point, that if I was going to be a successful saver, I would have to start small. Even if you can only afford to put $10 into your savings account every two weeks, that's still better than nothing! Start small, and build up with time.

Step 5: Maximize Your Interest

If you happen to have a healthy savings account, your bank may have already asked you about receiving higher interest payments. This is definitely something to discuss with your favorite teller if you haven't already. Essentially, if you don't plan on touching your savings account, you can earn higher interest in it. This could end up helping you save a lot more money in the long run.

Step 6: Stash Your Windfall Profits

Most young people (especially those who earn a low income) receive a rather hefty tax refund every year, which oftentimes inspires impulse shopping. Instead of using your tax refund to buy a new computer or adopt another cat, consider putting that money into your emergency savings account instead. This will be a great way to ensure that you have at least a couple hundred dollars in savings should you need it in the event of an emergency.

THE STORY OF ERICA WONG

After graduating from her university, Erica landed a job in her field (civil engineering), which was fantastic! She also had $90,000 in loans looming over her, which was not so fantastic. In order to tackle this situation, Erica had to dial back her lifestyle considerably. She did the math and realized that if she was going to pay off her loans in a timely manner (i.e. without accruing a ton of interest), she was going to have to learn to live on just

$13 a day. This was after paying off as many of her high-interest loans as she was able to and setting her low-interest loans up for automatic payment.

"I was miserable for the first year," Erica stated. She questioned why she went to work just to pay off student loans, and living on $13 a day obviously wasn't easy. She understood that paying off her loans would be necessary for her future though, so she persevered. She took it one month at a time, and was eventually able to pay off the last of her student loans after four and a half years of working. This was an enormous weight off her shoulders, and being debt-free would allow her to start saving up for her retirement.

As you can see, saving up money and digging yourself out of debt takes a lot of grit and determination. If you keep your eyes on the prize, though — like Erica did — you can get out of debt and start saving for your future.

THE STORY OF DAN AND CADY

Dan and Cady bought their first house after saving for more than two years. Like most people, however, they had to take out a mortgage loan right away, which came out to $146,000. This meant that their monthly payments were typically around $1,300. Obviously, $1,300 can be expensive for some, but Dan and Cady were smart savers. They set up a "house fund" before buying their home, which was how they were able to save up $46,000 for a down payment. From there, they started living by the "pay yourself first" principle, which meant they added to their house fund and their emergency fund every week before paying for anything else.

The couple also cut all unnecessary spending. Instead of going to Starbucks several times a week, they took an annual vacation — which ended up being a much better use of their time and money. The house they bought was also well within their means, so they were able to live quite comfortably despite having debts to pay off. Dan and Cady intend to be debt-free in just a couple of years, at which point they'll be able to invest in their financial future and retirement fund.

I'm sharing these stories now because I want to show you that saving for your future is possible if you're willing to put in the work and make certain sacrifices. It may not be easy at first, but again, you've got to think long-term. If you start saving now, the chances that you'll have to worry much about money in the future will lessen significantly. Trust the process. Erica, Dan, and Cady did.

INTERACTIVE ELEMENT

- Building up an emergency fund is crucial. It's generally recommended that you put three to six months' worth of your income into an emergency savings account. That way, you won't have to worry about money if something happens.
- Even if it's just $20, putting a set amount of money into your savings account each week is a great way to start saving for your future. That money will start to add up eventually, so stick with it!
- If you want to be a successful saver, you've got to make sacrifices. This might mean going out to eat less often or taking fewer trips to the mall. Consider how much you typically spend on your wants vs. your needs and adjust your spending habits accordingly.
- Don't wait to start saving up! The best way to save up lots of money for your retirement is the start saving while you're still young.

SEGUE

Saving up is challenging, but if you have more money coming in, it can make the process easier and provide you with more wiggle room. How do you make more money when you already have a job, you might ask? By making a passive income, of course! In the next chapter, I'll go over passive income streams and the ways in which earning passive income can help you gain financial independence more quickly.

6

ACTION STEP 5: CREATE ADDITIONAL PASSIVE INCOME STREAMS

M aking a decent income while also saving money takes a considerable amount of time-management skills. There are only so many hours in a single day, and most people spend the majority of each day earning an active income. What if there was a way to make even more money *while* working your day job, though? I know what you're thinking: how am I supposed to make more money while working? How would one even go about doing that? What if I don't have the time or energy to take on more work?

This is where earning a passive income can come in handy. Setting yourself up to earn a passive income (i.e. selling your intellectual property online or renting out a room in your house on Airbnb) means you'll be able to make money without having to do much of anything (other than the initial setup, of course). It's generally very easy to set yourself up to earn passive income, although a lot of passive income earners don't earn enough to support themselves by way of passive income alone. Try to think of your passive income source as a side gig that you don't have to put as much effort into. You'll be making money passively while earning money actively — which is a fantastic way to save up for your retirement or emergency fund.

The nice thing about having a passive income is you'll no longer have to depend on your active income to keep you afloat. Earning a passive income can be an especially great thing if you fall ill and need to take an extended period of time off from your day job. Even when you're not working, you'll be earning an income, which can be very relieving for people who struggle with chronic illnesses, mental health issues, and other disabilities.

Check out what Metrobank has to say about passive income: "When you have passive income, you're no longer solely dependent on your active income to cover for your living expenses. Passive income sources let you profit whether you're employed or not. Some passive income types can be lucrative, such as renting out properties you own where tenants are required to pay you monthly."

While some forms of passive income are liveable (i.e. renting out properties and charging your tenants monthly rent), you should try to keep in mind that most types of passive income are hit or miss opportunities. You might be successful selling your short stories online, or you might not. You might sell a million copies of your self-published e-book, or you might not. The truth is, you just never know. For this reason, I recommend sticking with your day job until you're sure that your passive income source will provide you with more than enough income to support yourself. I should know... I personally quit my full-time job several times pre-maturely and had to find another job to support my family before my passive income took off.

It's a good idea to make an active income and a passive income at the same time anyway, if you're able to do so. As I mentioned earlier, earning a passive income is going to allow you to have a bit more wiggle room, both work-wise and budget-wise. Those who earn a passive income are much more likely to be able to retire early due to the financial freedom their passive income has given them. If you've been feeling a lack of security and stability with your finances lately, setting yourself up to earn a passive income might just be the solution you've been looking for.

Once you gain a deeper understanding of passive income, you should have an easier time setting yourself up to earn it. Let's go over the main differences between passive and active income below, as well as the various benefits of earning a passive income. At the end of this chapter, you'll have an opportunity to brainstorm some action steps that will allow you to start creating one or two additional passive income streams. Let's get into it!

PASSIVE VS. ACTIVE INCOME

We briefly went over active income in Chapter 3, but a little refresher can't hurt. Active income earners are typically part-time or full-time workers, which includes freelancers and contractual workers. Earning an active income means performing a service or task within a certain amount of time, and getting paid for your work after the fact. Sources of income such as commissions and the tips you take home after each shift also counts as active income.

The great thing about earning an active income is it's a constant and reliable source of money. As long as you're able to work, you'll get a paycheck every two weeks (although, some active income earners do get paid weekly or per project). A lot of active income earners are not paid enough to be able to afford how they would like to live, however, which means many people end up taking second jobs or side gigs. *Or*, they set themselves up to earn passive income.

Now, passive income is a little bit more complicated than active income. The main idea behind earning a passive income is that you're "making money work for you." Earning a passive income often involves investing your money or selling work you've done in the past in order to make a profit. You work very hard on the front-end to be able to relax once things are built or you buy a system to where you are not directly involved to make a passive income, which is why many people feel it's preferable to make a passive income.

That said, it can be difficult to make a passive income — especially one that you can actually support yourself on. Not everyone is artistically talented, and most people don't have a spare room or mother-in-law apartment that they can rent out to tenants for passive income. Becoming a best-selling author is a one-in-a-million chance, as is being a successful social media influencer. And to be honest, most people are not willing to do what it takes to position themselves for success. However, if you have the opportunity to set up a source of passive income for yourself, you need to at least try! It may take years to build a substantial passive income, but it'll still take some of the turmoil out of budgeting and saving — no matter how much you end up making.

A Deeper Look at Passive Income

You've probably heard the phrase "time is money" before. Well, that doesn't necessarily apply to passive income. Earning a passive income involves creating or investing in a particular asset, which you can then sell or slowly generate earnings with. Typically, you can earn a passive income from anywhere, especially with automation and remote work gaining popularity. Most of the time, in order to earn a passive income, you need to do a decent amount of work up front. Writing a book is no easy task, and renting out property comes with its own set of challenges.

Once you get your passive income source up and running, however, you shouldn't have to do very much work at all. Yes, you may have to promote your book, photography, or art if you decide to sell it online, but that's mainly a waiting game. That's the other thing you should keep in mind about passive income. I've said it once already and I'll say it again: *building passive income takes time!*

With passive income, you have to know that all of your hard work will eventually pay off and you will know by the passion you have for the business you are creating. As I said before, sometimes it does and sometimes it doesn't. Most of the time, though, the benefits of earning a passive income will make your efforts well worth it in the end. Let's take a look at some of the different types of passive income you can earn below.

THE DIFFERENT TYPES OF PASSIVE INCOME

You can earn a passive income in one of two ways (or, you can do both!): creating and/or investing. Both forms of passive income can be risky, but if you're successful, you can end up earning some serious cash. When selling your art or investing in stocks, you'll want to make sure that you're earning an active income at the same time. This will ensure that you'll have money on hand, just in case your passive income source doesn't take off right away. Creating is not an option for everyone, nor is investing. I'd like to go over both in a bit more detail in hopes that gaining a solid under-standing of both will help you make your passive income source decision.

Creating

A friend of mine, Cassandra has a master's degree in creative writing. She's currently churning out a series of mystery-horror novellas as her main source of passive income. Cassandra also works at a restaurant full-time, which she doesn't particularly enjoy, but it pays the bills. She once told me that the number one thing people ask her when they find out that she writes and self-publishes books is this: "do you make a lot of money doing that?" Cassandra supposes people ask it because they're interested in writing and self-publishing as well.

"I don't make enough to support myself on writing alone," she always tells them. "But I make enough to supplement my income and save for my retirement." The thing about Cassandra is, she *loves* writing, so creating this book series has allowed to her make money doing something she actually enjoys — which is something many people strive for but are never actually able to achieve. Granted, it's hard! It took years for Cassandra to build up a fan base for her books, and in the beginning, things felt pretty bleak. She kept with it, though, and is now making passive income from books she wrote years ago. Creating (and selling) art isn't easy, but if you have the time and determination, you can definitely make money doing it. Give it a try sometime if you want to see it for yourself.

Investing

Now, technically speaking, you're more likely to make medium to long-term money investing than you are creating. That said, you're also more likely to *lose* money — especially if the stock market is unstable (spoiler alert: the stock market is usually unstable). I'm not saying that investing in stocks is a bad thing, but it's essentially like gambling. There's a high-risk, high-reward/low-risk, low-reward factor depending on what you are doing. When investing in stocks as a beginner, you should avoid individual stocks. While you can get lucky (like a gambler in a casino), you're much more likely to experience a downturn due to the stock market's constant fluctuation.

If you have money to invest, you should go ahead and invest it. Just know that (as with all forms of passive income), there's a risk that comes with investing. If you decide to invest in, say, a particular brand of lemonade and a hurricane hits the orchard where the lemons are harvested, the stock market could take a dive — which means you'll lose whatever you previously invested. Honestly, it's a good idea to try out a stock market simulator before investing any real money in stocks. If you're familiar with Nintendo's *Animal Crossing: New Horizons*, you know all about the "stalk" market (for those who don't know, you play with turnip stalks). You invest in turnips and make a profit by selling them to the Nook twins, or you end up with a bunch of moldy turnips if things don't end up working out in your favor.

HOW MUCH CAN YOU MAKE FROM PASSIVE INCOME?

There's not really a limit to how much you can make from passive income. You might make an extra 10 cents a month, or you might make an extra thousand dollars a month. It can depend on a variety of factors, including the value of the product you're selling, how much you're selling it for, and the amount of time, effort, and resources you put into building this particular source of passive income in the first place. Again, when it comes to passive income, you just won't know until you try.

EXAMPLES OF PASSIVE INCOME

We've already gone over a few examples of passive income, but I'd like to delve into more detail regarding some of the most common ways people go about earning a passive income during their daily lives. Most of these methods involve investing time or money in one way or another, so just be prepared to do so.

Owning a Business

Depending on how you build up your business, owning one might be a passive activity. As an independent writer, for instance, you're exchanging your labor for money, which is not a passive activity. On the flip side, if you're a creator or producer, you can profit from affiliate marketing and digital goods to make passive revenue. Allowing other businesses to use their creations will allow performers and artists to receive compensation. You could also invest in an established company that generates regular income and start making money right away. The choice is up to you.

Rental Income

Real estate is where more millionaires have been made and where monthly revenue is generated. It frequently entails purchasing real estate and lending it to a renter. Some believe that renting out property isn't inactive because you have to keep it up to date and manage it. However, if you want someone to look after the house, apartment, or room you're lending out, you could always hire a property manager to handle things. Alternatively, you can invest a few hours each month into handling inquiries and issues from your tenants. When a tenant vacates and a new one comes in, this is when rental revenue requires the greatest time commitment.

Private Equity

Whatever money you invest into a business or real estate is referred to as private equity. These ventures are typically seen as hazardous, and the majority of them demand substantial funds. Private equity assets are frequently held by investors for anywhere from one to ten years. On the other hand, if you're looking for a long-term investment, they could end up being a decent source of passive income.

Stock Market

Investing in the stock market is one of the most popular ways to earn a passive income. Basically, companies return gains to stockholders in the form of dividends as they make profits. You can engage in a range of products that pay dividends, including equity dividends, index funds, and dividend exchange-traded funds. Investing in the stock market is surprisingly easy, but as I discussed earlier, it doesn't come without its risks.

THE BENEFITS OF PASSIVE INCOME

There's nothing wrong with wanting to make a little extra cash on the side or even building a very profitable business. In fact, most people jump at the chance to work a side gig, or — even better — generate passive income. There are plenty of benefits to earning a passive income, most notably increased financial stability, more financial freedom, and reduced reliance on your active income paycheck. Let's go over some of the main benefits of earning a passive income in a bit more detail below.

You'll Have More Financial Stability

Plenty of young people work hard to secure their financial futures. Oftentimes, they find themselves pinching pennies and living paycheck to paycheck. This doesn't have to be you, though! When you're making a passive income, you don't have to worry so much about whether or not you'll have enough money to pay rent each month. You'll also gain financial security much more quickly because you'll be aware of your financial safety net.

You Won't Have to Rely Solely on a Paycheck

A lot of young people depend on their salary to cover their monthly rent and other expenses. Problems may arise if your compensation is less than usual as a result of sick leave or vacation time. However, this is not a concern when you're making a passive income. With passive income streams, you'll always have money coming in, which you'll be able to use for emergency purposes if need be. You'll also be able to take more vacation days, which is definitely a plus!

You'll Be Able to Meet Your Financial Goals

Naturally, earning a passive income will provide you with access to more money. This means that you'll have extra money to place into your savings account, which in turn will help you prepare for significant expenses — such as a car, a home, college tuition, or early retirement. In a nutshell, earning a passive income will help you achieve your financial goals more quickly.

You'll Gain Location Independence

Have you ever envisioned how wonderful it would be to earn money while lounging on a beach in Cancun or the Maldives? After all, we frequently observe prominent personalities and social media influencers doing it! With a passive income, you can start traveling the world and still make money at times when you aren't required to be at work. You'll have the flexibility to work and reside wherever you want thanks to passive income! This is probably my favorite thing about passive income. I do not mind sending an email or taking a quick call while I'm sitting on the beach with my family or watching the sun rise in the mountains because of the freedom I have to do so.

You'll Be Able to Retire Early

Many people eagerly anticipate their retirement, especially those who have been working for a long time. However, if you're currently living paycheck-to-paycheck, retirement might be something that's difficult for you to envision. The good news is you can start preparing for retirement earlier if you have a passive income. This will enable you to appreciate your senior years and retire much sooner.

HOW TO CREATE PASSIVE INCOME

Now that you've learned about passive income, you're on the right track to creating a source of passive income for yourself. There are a number of ways you can go about setting up a passive income source, including:

Creating a Course

Making an audio or video course, then sitting back and watching the money come in is a common method people use to generate passive income. Sites like Udemy, SkillShare, and Kajabi allow for the distribution and sale of courses, so the process isn't too difficult at all! This can also be a great opportunity to teach people all about something you're passionate about (while making money at the same time).

Writing an eBook

This can be a good way to benefit from the cheap cost of self-publication. You can even use Amazon's global marketing to get your book in front of possibly millions of potential customers. Since they depend on your own expertise, ebooks can be created for comparatively little money. Just keep in mind that if you're going to write an ebook, you need to do the research or you need to be an authority on a particular subject. That said, fiction sells as well!

Rental Income

Renting out properties to tenants can be a particularly lucrative passive income-earning method. However, it usually requires a lot more work than most people expect. You've got to maintain the property you invested in and consider that some tenants may pay late or cause irreparable damages — which means your money will essentially be going down the drain. It can absolutely be worth it, though, especially if you learn how to pick your tenants carefully.

Flipping Retail Products

Use online marketplaces like eBay or Amazon to your benefit and resell items you discover elsewhere for a discount. You can make money by negotiating the difference between your buying and selling prices, and you might even develop a following of people who keep track of your deals. The price discrepancies between what you can find and what the typical customer might be able to find will allow you to profit. If you have a friend who can give you access to discounted goods that few other people are likely to discover, this might work particularly well for you.

Sell Your Photography Online

128 | KIRK TEACHOUT

Although selling photographs online might not seem like the most obvious option when it comes to starting a passive income stream, you might be able to expand your efforts if you can sell the same images repeatedly. You could collaborate with a company like Shutterstock, or Alamy if you want to accomplish that. It's important to keep in mind that you must first receive platform approval before you can start licensing your photographs for use by anyone who buys them. When someone utilizes your picture on the platform, you'll get paid in passive income.

INTERACTIVE ELEMENT

Use the space below to brainstorm and write down some action steps you want to take in regard to creating your own passive income streams:

SEGUE

In the next chapter, we'll go over the basics of investing and why it's so important for young people to be able to effectively analyze investment opportunities. It's easy to make mistakes while investing, after all — unless you know how to avoid making the following common mistakes.

7

ACTION STEP 6: INVEST YOUR MONEY

Investing your money can be scary at first, but if you know how to go about it the right way, the payoff can be tremendous. When it comes to making investments, the earlier you start the better. That said, you want to be sure that you're absolutely ready. After all, the last thing you want to do is invest your money without fully understanding what you're doing! The investing process can be complicated and is oftentimes lifelong, which is why I feel it may be beneficial to discuss the ins and outs of investing in this chapter.

Some people decide not to invest at all within their life-times because they're afraid of the risks associated with investing. This is fine (to each their own), but consider this: if you never take any risks, you'll never gain any potential benefits either. This goes for *everything* in life, not just investing your money. You don't necessarily want to go overboard with taking this particular type of risk — and you should never invest *all* of your money — but in the long run, investing can be a great way to generate a whole lot of extra cash. So, why not give it a try?

Consider what Merril — a Bank of America company — has to say about investing: "It's best to start saving and investing as soon as you start earning money, even if it's only $10 a paycheck. The discipline and skills you learn can benefit you for the rest of your life. But no matter how old you are when you start thinking seriously about saving and investing, it's never too late to begin." If you're currently earning an active and/or passive income, what's stopping you from saving and making investments? It's awfully easy to get stuck in a rut, but if you're interested in saving and investing more money for your future, you should probably start now.

My friends older brother, Michael, used to work with someone who would constantly bring up his stocks over lunch. Michael had a 401(k) at the time, but he wasn't particularly interested in the stock market. After some urging from his coworker, however, he eventually began investing his money, at first contributing only $100 per month, then, several years later, $500 per quarter while periodically adding extra funds as time went by. Since then, his investments have become his biggest asset. He was even able to remodel his house last year as an anniversary gift to his wife. Because things worked out so well for my brother, he should be able to retire early — all because he took a chance and invested in the stock market!

Of course, not everyone who invests in stocks has a success story like Michael's, but if Michael hadn't invested in stocks, he'd probably be living a very different life right now. There is risk involved in every investment. In order to determine how much risk your investments should bear, you must weigh your ability to endure price fluctuations against the necessary rate of return. Time is a counterbalancing element to risk. If you intend to maintain an investment for a long period of time, you might be more willing to take on certain risks because you'll have more time to recover from any early losses. It's definitely a good idea to take on less risk and have more liquidity in your assets when making a shorter-term commitment, like saving for a home or second car, for instance.

At this point, you might be thinking: "investing sounds way too complicated and risky. Why can't I just have a savings account?" You absolutely can just have a savings account — no one is going to stop you from doing whatever you want with your money — but you've got to keep your best interest and your future in mind. Most would agree that it's in your best interest to have a savings account *and* investments lined up. Having one or the other is better than nothing, but it's ultimately not enough. Let me show you what I mean.

WHY SHOULD YOU INVEST?

Have you ever heard "The Grain of Rice" fable from India? Sometimes, stories can help us understand complicated concepts better, so I'll reiterate the fable below (just to keep things a bit more concise).

A long time ago in India, there was a king who thought himself to be intelligent and just, as a raja ought to be. His region was populated by rice growers. Everyone was required by the raja's order to give him almost all of their rice. The raja assured the people, "I will keep the rice safe and secure, so that in times of hunger, everyone will have rice to consume, and no one will go without it." Nearly all of the rice produced by the growers was gathered annually by the raja's rice collectors, who then transported it to the royal storehouses.

The rice grew well for several seasons. The storehouses were always filled because citizens donated almost all of their rice to the raja. The only thing remaining for everyone else was just enough rice to survive on. The following year, the rice developed blight and the crop failed — causing famine and starvation. The people lacked both rice to consume and rice to offer to the raja. "Your highness, let us open the royal storehouses and give the rice to the people, as you promised," the raja's officials beseeched him. The king cried: "No! Promise or no promise, a raja must not go hungry!"

As time passed, the population's hunger increased. However, the king refused to distribute any rice. As a raja should, even in times of famine, he demanded a feast one day for himself and his advisors. Two full baskets of rice were carried by an elephant, led by the raja's servant from the storehouse to his palace. A small stream of rice was trickling out from one of the baskets, which a young girl called Rani noticed. She stood up and walked next to the elephant while collecting the rice in her skirt. Clever girl that she was, she began to come up with a plan.

When the palace guard saw Rani doing this, he called her a thief. She explained that she was not a thief and that she was simply catching the rice that fell so that she may return it to the raja. When the raja heard about this, he was delighted. He told her: "I wish to reward you for returning what belongs to me. Ask me for anything, and you shall have it." The girl told him that she didn't deserve any reward at all, but requested a single grain of rice.

This seemed far too modest a reward to the raja, so he said: "Surely you will allow me to reward you more plentifully, as a raja should." Rani pleased that her plan had worked, replied: "Very well. If it pleases Your Highness, you may reward me in this way. Today, you will give me a single grain of rice. Then, each day for thirty days you will give me double the rice you gave me the day before. Thus, tomorrow you will give me two grains of rice, the next day four grains of rice, and so on for thirty days."

The raja agreed, though he was a bit confused because this reward still seemed quite modest. Naturally, the rice gifted to Rani began to add up significantly. On the thirtieth day, 236 elephants traversed the province, hauling 5,368,709 grains of rice — four royal store-houses worth! Rani had accumulated more than five million grains of rice by that time. In the end, the king had no more rice to give to her. Bested, he sighed. "What will you do with this rice?" he asked her.

"I shall give it to all the hungry people," Rani told him. "and I shall leave a basket of rice for you, too, if you promise, from now on, to take only as much rice as you need." The raja promised — and stuck to his promise — as a raja should.

As you can see, in this story, Rani made a smart investment. The raja didn't have an understanding of compound interest, so he just assumed the rice he would have to gift to Rani would remain a small amount over time. The moral of this story is: don't make risky investments with money that you can't afford to lose. When making investments, you want your money to be safe and you want it to grow. The more potential there is for growth in an investment, the more risky the investment will be.

Making a smart investment is essentially the same thing as not putting all of your eggs in one basket. If you don't transport all of your eggs in one basket, you're far less likely to lose all of your eggs at once (from say, tripping and falling, or the basket breaking from the weight of the eggs). Hopefully, this story has provided you with a decent example of how to make a good investment. Let's get into the main reasons why you should invest your money below:

Having a Savings Account Isn't Enough

Although having a savings account is crucial, it's not the only course of action you should take if you want to increase your savings. Smart savers will work to gather enough disaster or emergency funds in a savings account while also investing in a money market account. As we've already discussed, investing in the stock market can provide you with a number of possible benefits once three to six months' worth of easily accessible savings has been accumulated.

Why Investing Matters

Not everyone considers investing their money because of the risk factor involved, but investing has worked well for years for many people all over the world. It can be an exceptionally powerful way to use your money to increase your savings. The great thing about investing is, your money may end up increasing in value, which means inflation won't affect you much as long as you're able to make wise investment decisions. The powerful effects of compounding and the trade-off between risk and yield are the main reasons investing has such a high money development potential. In other words, investing is absolutely worth it!

The Power of Compounding

Rani clearly understood the power of compounding. When a particular dividend (or profits from a property) are returned, compounding takes place. These profits or rewards then produce more profits. In other words, compounding occurs when your assets produce income from earnings that you've already generated. For instance, if you invest in a stock that pays dividends, you might think about reinvesting those dividends to increase the possible power of compounding.

If I gave you the choice between $1,000,000 today or a penny that doubled every day for 30 days, which would you choose? If you doubled a single cent each day, you'd have $5,368,709.12 by day 30. That's compounding at work! However, you should keep in mind that not everything depends on the power of doubling. For example, if you modified the doubling period to just 27 days and posed the same question I just asked you, you would only have $671,088.64.

The Risk-Return Tradeoff

The possible return and market risk of various investments tend to differ based on several factors. Market risk is the possibility that a venture will end up bringing in a lower return than anticipated — or even lose value. Return is the amount of money you make based on the assets you've invested, or the total value growth of a particular investment. Purchasing stocks has the potential to yield greater profits. In comparison, although it's thought to be less risky than dealing in stocks, money market or savings account investments probably won't yield the same results.

INVESTMENT TYPES FOR BEGINNERS

If you're feeling intimidated by the idea of investing your money, you're definitely not alone. Perhaps you've heard investment horror stories from your friends or relatives, or maybe you just don't like the idea of potentially losing your hard-earned cash — which is totally understandable!

It's important that you don't get too preoccupied with whether or not this is the ideal moment to begin investing in stocks. You will undoubtedly come across a variety of market environments throughout your investing career. It's crucial for novice investors to understand the risk level of certain investments before making any investments whatsoever. Some assets are riskier than others, and you don't want to encounter a nasty surprise after you've already invested your money. Take your ability to go without the funds you'll be investing into consideration. You will need to be able to go a few years or longer without having access to them.

No one teaches you about making smart investments in high school, which is why I'm here to show you the ropes. Let's take a closer look at some of the investment types you should be taking an interest in as a beginner.

High-Yield Savings Accounts

This may be one of the easiest methods you can use to increase your investment return over that of a normal checking account. High-yield savings accounts, which are frequently established through an online bank, typically offer clients regular access to their funds while paying an average interest rate that's higher than that of a standard savings account. This can be a fantastic spot to stash money you're holding onto in case of an emergency.

Certificates of Deposit (CDs)

An alternative to high-yield savings accounts is a certificate of deposit (CD), however, investing in this will lock up your money for an extended period of time. You can buy a CD for as little as six months or as long as five years, but usually, you can't access the money before the CD expires without generating fees. CDs are thought to be very secure, and if you buy one from a bank that's nationally insured, you'll be covered for up to $250,000 per depositor, per proprietorship.

401(k) or a Similar Workplace Retirement Plan

This may be among the easiest methods to begin investing, and it comes with a few major advantages that may help you both now and in the future. The majority of employers offer to match a part of the amount you decide to set aside from your normal paycheck for retirement. In other words, you are passing up free money if your company offers a match and you don't take advantage of the opportunity. Contributions to a conventional 401(k) are made before taxes are due, and they increase tax-free until you reach retirement age. Some companies provide Roth 401(k)s, which enable post-tax payments. You won't have to pay taxes on payments made during retirement if you choose this option.

Mutual Funds

Investors who may not be able to readily put together a portfolio of stocks, bonds, or other assets on their own will be given the chance to do so through mutual funds. The most well-liked mutual funds follow benchmarks like the S&P 500, which includes 500 of the biggest U.S. corporations. Investors in index funds typically pay very little or no expenses, depending on the fund. These affordable fees enable buyers to retain a larger portion of the fund returns, which can be a great way to accumulate wealth over time.

ETFs

While exchange-traded funds (or ETFs) move throughout the day as stocks do, they differ from mutual funds in that they contain an array of securities. The minimal investment for ETFs is lower than that of mutual funds (usually a few thousand dollars). ETFs can be bought for the price of one share plus any applicable fees or charges, though you can start out with even less if your broker supports fractional share trading. In tax-advantaged accounts like 401(k)s and IRAs, mutual funds and exchange-traded funds (ETFs) make excellent investments.

Individual Stocks

This is the riskiest investing strategy I'll be talking about here (although, this strategy can also be one of the most lucrative). You should always think about whether purchasing a stock makes sense for you before you start making individual investments. Ask yourself whether you truly understand the company you're investing in and whether or not you're investing for the long term, which is typically defined as at least five years. Because stocks are priced every single second of the trading day, people who own individual stocks frequently succumb to the short-term trading mindset.

It's generally a better idea to think about using the more diversified strategy provided by mutual funds or exchange-traded funds, especially if you don't believe you have the knowledge or stamina to fight it out with specific stocks.

HOW TO GET STARTED

Now for the exciting part: getting your investment process started! No matter where you put your money into investments, it's important to keep in mind that you are basically providing it to a business, the government, or another organization in the hopes that they will give you more money in the future. The majority of the time, when people invest money, they have a particular objective in mind — such as early retirement, a new home, or their children's future education.

Trading and saving money is not the same thing as investing it. Investing typically involves setting money aside for a long time as opposed to trading stocks on the regular. Saving money is also safer than investing. Investments are not always protected, but savings usually are. That said, you would never have more money than what you already have saved for yourself if you kept your money hidden away and didn't invest it.

THINGS TO CONSIDER BEFORE INVESTING

First and foremost, it's a good idea to ask yourself a few key questions before you start making investments. For instance, do you owe a lot of money on your credit cards? If you answered "yes" to this question, you're probably not ready to make an investment just yet. Before making an investment, you'll want to do everything in your power to pay off your credit card debt. It's important to remember that no investment will ever reliably outperform the 26% or so APR that you're probably paying a credit card company to maintain your debt — so just keep that in mind.

The second thing you'll want to ask yourself is: do you have an emergency fund saved up? As I mentioned previously, life happens and will continue to happen. Layoffs, natural disasters, and sudden illnesses can end up turning your life upside down. Any financial professional will tell you that you should have between six months and a year's worth of living expenses in your savings account in case an emergency occurs. By having this money saved up, you'll be able to escape complete ruin if worse comes to worst.

BEGINNERS INVESTING TIPS

Investing is what you do when you have some money left over at the end of the month after all your other expenses have been taken care of. If you haven't been saving your money, you're not ready to invest. Once you have some funds saved up, you should start investing immediately. Usually, the interest rate on a savings account will not be able to keep up with rising inflation. In actuality, you'll be making savings while also losing money. Unfortunately, that's the cost of having cash on hand. For this reason, you ought to begin making investments as soon as possible.

You should also have an understanding of what you're investing in — an investment goal, if you will. You might be investing money to pay for your future child's impending college expenses, for example. You may want to invest money now so you have it when you retire later on. Each of these assets has a very distinct timeframe. It's important to keep in mind that some assets will be more important to you than others in the future. Investors with limited time should be more cautious as well. Riskier assets are typically more available to those who are investing money they won't need for a while. Just some food for thought!

WHAT TO AVOID AS AN INVESTMENT NEWBIE

As a new investor, you're likely to make a few mistakes when you're first starting out. This is totally normal, and thankfully, there are ways you can avoid making absolutely drastic investing mistakes. It's always good to be aware, so let's go over some of the main mistakes investment newbies make below:

Investing Before You're Ready

Remember: don't start investing your money until you've got a healthy amount built up in your savings account for emergencies and other future expenses. It's also not a good idea to start making investments if you've got a lot of credit card or student loan debt to pay off. You want to be completely ready — mentally and financially — before you start investing.

Setting Unrealistic Expectations

Investing in the stock market can be a slow process for accumulating wealth, and any hopes for fast profit can easily come to an abrupt end. You should never invest any funds that you might need within the next five years in stocks because the market periodically falls and can take several years to rebound.

Trusting the Wrong People

Many new investors place far too much trust in financial TV programs or popular stock recommendations from friends or family members. Anybody can suggest a company, but you hardly ever know the recommender's track record, and even the best investors occasionally make mistakes. Remember the story I told you about my friend's brother? He invested in stocks because his coworker urged him to, but he definitely, *definitely* got lucky.

Paying Too Much in Commissions

Make sure not to overspend on trading commissions when you start investing your money. Aim to pay fees that are no more than 2% of the trade's worth. For example, you should pay no more than $20 in fees on a transaction of $1,000. Nowadays, many reputable brokerages charge $7 or less per transaction. Watch out for brokerages that are predatory!

Not Diversifying Sufficiently

Another frequent investing mistake is under-diversifying, which isn't always remedied by holding a large number of different stocks. You are not very diversified if say, 10 of your stocks are energy firms and 10 are tech companies. You should try to invest across a variety of industries and, ideally, across multiple nations. Focus on American stocks if you want, but you might also want to add some foreign investments once you get the hang of things.

THE STORY OF WARREN BUFFET

Warren Buffet is one of the richest men in the world. Obviously, he's led a pretty successful life! Like most people, Warren Buffet wasn't born rich. He was an everyday person, just like you or me. How, then, did he become one of the most successful investors of all time? Well, he would probably tell you himself that the process wasn't easy.

Like most successful investors, Warren Buffet had to risk everything to achieve his gain in life. He started working for Benjamin Graham, who was considered to be the father of value investing. In the early 1950s, Buffet learned how to spot especially promising net-net stocks (as opposed to cheap ones). Using Graham's strategies and teachings, he took a simple approach with his investments — which is how he got to where he is today. But, most importantly, it took consistency and time.

In short, making smart investments is all about understanding the stock market and thinking carefully about your options before making investment choices. Warren Buffet did, and you can too!

INTERACTIVE ELEMENT

- It's important that you pay off your credit card and student loan debts before you start investing your money in stocks.
- One of the most common mistakes new investors make is paying too much in commissions. Commission fees for stocks should not be higher than 2%.
- Investing in stocks is risky if you don't understand exactly what you're doing. It will help to have a good understanding of compound interest. You should also make sure that you're sufficiently researching the stocks you're most interested in investing in.
- The earlier you're able to start investing, the better!

SEGUE

We are nearly at the end now. In the final chapter, we'll go over the importance of reevaluating your financial goals and savings progress on a regular basis. You've worked hard to get to where you are, but there are some things you'll need to do if you want to continue to succeed financially.

8

ACTION STEP 7: REEVALUATE YOUR FINANCIAL GOALS REGULARLY

Life tends to be turbulent and unpredictable, especially once you reach adulthood. Your life circumstances can end up changing significantly — and so can your financial goals as a direct result. The truth is, you never know what life is going to throw at you. Trying to have one baby could result in you having triplets as my friends did. If you don't have good health insurance, impromptu hospital visits could end up throwing a wrench into your plans. This is why it's a good idea to keep your financial plans flexible (or at least review and reevaluate them once in a while).

You might be thinking to yourself: I've been doing fine, financially. Do I really need to review my financial goals? What does it really mean to review my financial goals, anyway? What does that even entail? Don't worry, because I'm here to answer all of these questions in this chapter! Check out this quote from PNC: "What is needed for a financial review? An updated financial statement that includes assets, liabilities and cash from the previous year, as well as plans for what you want to accomplish. Questions and concerns based on that financial statement. Account statements and other information related to investments, inventory, assets and debts."

Now, this might sound like kind of a lot, but conducting regular financial reviews is well worth your time. Let's say, for example, you decide to do an annual financial review with a financial advisor (which is the route most people take). Conducting a yearly annual review is just as important as going to your yearly health physical. You wouldn't neglect your physical or mental health, and you shouldn't neglect your financial health either. If going through an annual financial review sounds a bit cumbersome and overwhelming to you, you're not alone. Let's dive into the ins and out of financial goal reviews below, just to simplify things a little.

THE IMPORTANCE OF REGULAR FINANCIAL GOAL REVIEWS

Proper financial planning entails much more than just coming up with a strategy. To ensure that you're spending effectively and prudently, frequent evaluation is absolutely necessary. It's essential to conduct frequent financial reviews because your personal circumstances don't always stay the same. Your salary may increase or decrease, and your mindset toward financial risk may change as a result. There are endless reasons why conducting regular financial goal reviews is so important, but the main reasons are listed below:

Evaluate Your Attitude Toward Risk

Understanding your mindset toward investment risk is essential when it comes to successful financial planning. Whether you're aware of it or not, the risk is often linked to your current situation (i.e. the job you're working, the salary you're making, you're current expenses, etc.). By routinely examining your situation, you'll have the chance to adjust what stocks and shares you're investing in based on your attitude toward risk at that particular moment. Risk can change quite quickly based on your dependents, age, work stability, and a variety of other factors.

Keeps Your Plan Effective and Relevant

Life is unpredictable. Changes could occur at any time, and these changes could end up having a significant impact on your financial position and future. You need to review your future financial objectives on a regular basis in order to make sure your financial strategy is still effective and applicable in the face of changes in relationships, employment, family size, and anything else.

Invest Your Money in the Right Places

Maybe your employer has increased your salary or given you a bonus recently, and now you have more money to spend. Perhaps a departed family member left you an inheritance or your wealthy grandmother sent you a huge check. By conducting regular financial reviews, you'll be able to ensure that your financial strategy is taking events like these into account and that you're making the right choices when choosing where to invest your money.

The Wider Economy

There are a lot of unpredictability factors that can impact the investments you make over time, and you never know what sort of effects these factors could have on you personally — from laws influencing when you'll be eligible for your pension/retirement funds when you reach retirement to changes in tax allowances. You'll be in a better position to react to possible opportunities and evaluate potential risks if you regularly review your financial plan.

Improves Your Confidence and Understanding

Speaking with a dependable adviser about your money can boost your self-confidence and help you comprehend various investments, benefits, and their broader consequences. Reviewing your financial plan will ultimately help you feel more confident about the choices you're making, as well as make you feel more at ease knowing that you're doing what needs to be done to achieve the future of your dreams.

HOW OFTEN SHOULD FINANCIAL REVIEWS HAPPEN?

It's a good idea to review your financial objectives every year. However, for some, yearly financial goal reviews might not be sufficient. When an emergency or unforeseen expense arises, you might not be able to take the necessary precautions to maintain a balanced budget and savings account. For example, what happens if you're unable to generate enough savings during the subsequent months to meet the financial goals you've set?

If you find yourself gradually withdrawing more money from your savings or checking account to pay off all of your various expenses, you might want to conduct a financial review. Every time you withdraw money from your savings account, you're unintentionally expanding your financial disparity. You might find that your budget plan has gone horribly awry at the close of the year, meaning it will be especially difficult to correct the issues at hand.

Of course, these things just happen sometimes. If you conduct more frequent financial reviews, however, you should be able to prevent falling into financial disparity the majority of the time. Particularly for those who are newly financially literate, it's a good idea to conduct quarterly financial reviews rather than annual ones. I personally go over my finances once a quarter to see if I'm on track and then meet with my financial advisor once a year.

Conducting Quarterly Financial Goal Check-Ups

If you're new to personal finance, you should start conducting fast financial check-ups every quarter rather than just once a year. This will enable you to assess your current expenses, and determine whether or not your income has changed. You'll also be able to gauge whether or not you're on schedule to reach your financial goals while also remaining within your budget. From there, you'll be able to take immediate steps to get back on track if you discover any hiccups in your financial plan. In order to conduct a quarterly financial check-up, you'll need to collect all of your account records from the previous three months. Examine your budget for any inconsistencies and make any necessary changes if you've happened to incur extra costs.

WHAT TO DO WHEN YOUR FINANCIAL GOALS FEEL UNREALISTIC

What are some of your main financial goals? Are you saving up for your dream home or planning for an early retirement? Do you want to be free from your credit card debt or travel the world someday? Despite the fact that these goals will take some time and planning, they're realistically achievable. Chances are you *will* get your dream home, your world travel experience, your early retirement, and your debt-free lifestyle — just as long as you're able to save, invest, and budget.

I'm not saying it's that simple, but it is realistic. When it comes to financial planning, it's important to be able to identify the difference between realistic financial goals and unrealistic financial goals. If any of your financial goals feel too big or generic, you might want to consider starting small. Achieving your small goals will eventually allow you to achieve your big goals. Just know that it might take a little while.

So, what should you do if your financial goals feel unrealistic? Let's go over a few action steps you can take below if you feel like you're financial plans haven't been working out very well lately:

Try to Determine What's Wrong

If your goal is to pay off all of your credit card debt within a calendar year or to save up enough money to buy a house by the time you're 22, you're going to want to sit down and do some reevaluation depending on your income. Conduct some thorough number-crunching and be sincere with yourself. You need to acknowledge whether the goal you've set is unachievable in this particular instance — especially if it requires you to make debt payments or save an amount of money that's greater than your income or monthly budget.

If this is the case, don't get discouraged. It's important to have this realization because it means you'll be able to reevaluate and revise some of your more unattainable goals. It's also important to keep in mind that your objectives might not always be feasible due to various circumstances. Are you overspending on eating out to the point where you aren't making enough monthly savings? Do you need to switch from part-time to full-time employment in order to make more money for your debt repayment goals? In these situations, you can make changes in order to refocus your goals.

Identify Ways to Deal With What's Standing in Your Way

Your goals may be impeded by certain obstacles, such as paying off student loans, or credit card debt. If your goals seem unattainable, consider whether these obstacles are keeping you from making progress in your financial future. You should take care of your debt first, for instance, if you're trying to save money for retirement. Your priorities should be rearranged so that you're devoting resources equally, if not more, to paying off debts so that you can concentrate on completing your goals for the future.

Set S.M.A.R.T. Financial Goals

S.M.A.R.T., in this context, stands for: Specific, Measurable, Attainable, Realistic, and Timely. Setting S.M.A.R.T. financial goals is all about keeping certain factors in mind whilst setting your goals. For example, what exactly is your goal? Do you have a specific amount of money in mind that you want to save or use to pay off your debts? Is the purpose of achieving this financial goal to pay off your credit cards or to start an emergency fund? How will you gauge your development? Will you assess your money position on a monthly or quarterly basis? It's important to ask yourself these types of questions if you're going to set S.M.A.R.T. financial goals for yourself!

Break Your Goals Into Smaller Chunks

Remember: it takes time to accomplish a significant life goal. It requires determination, commitment, and perseverance. If your goals are enormously high, like, for instance — wanting to save up $1 million in five years or attempting to retire in ten — they may seem unreachable. You might feel overwhelmed by a goal that's so difficult that you're unsure of where to begin. For this reason, it's a good idea to break up your financial goals into more manageable chunks. Perhaps you can save up $5,000 annually or add $100 to your retirement savings every month. Consider what works for you and remember to work within your budget.

Align Your Goals With Your Budget

Your budget will ultimately determine whether or not you're able to achieve your financial goals. The reason for this is that your budget includes all of your monthly expenses, from set costs like rent and utilities to unpredictable expenses like dining out, leisure, and emergency situations. It additionally helps you keep track of how much money you make each month. Your monthly budget needs to realistically and sustainably accommodate your financial goals. If your monthly savings goal is $400 but after paying your set expenses, your budget only leaves $375 available, your goal is unfortunately unrealistic.

Set up a Contingency Plan

Again, you never know what life is going to throw at you. For this reason, in case an unavoidable (and expensive) emergency happens, you're going to want to come up with a contingency plan. This could entail setting aside $50 per month for an emergency fund or reserving a small portion of your target funds for unexpected expenses. Knowing that you'll experience setbacks can be helpful, but what will keep you motivated and on schedule with your finances is having a strategy to deal with them when they occur.

INTERACTIVE ELEMENT

1. Why are frequent financial reviews important? (Circle all that apply)

    a. It ensures your financial plan remains relevant and effective
    b. It can improve your financial confidence
    c. You'll invest your money in the right places
    d. Financial reviews aren't all that important

2. How often should you conduct a financial review?

    a. Every day
    b. Once a month
    c. Once every three months
    d. Once every five years

3. What should you do if your financial goals feel unrealistic?

    a. Determine what's standing in your way

b. Ask your parents for money

c. Align your goals with your budget

d. Set up a backup plan

Answer Key:

1. a), b), and c)
2. b) and/or c)
3. a), c), and d)

SEGUE

You have now reached the end of this book! Give yourself a pat on the back. The next section will be a short refresher on everything you've learned over eight chapters, so I encourage you to read on!

CONCLUSION

Now that you're aware of the action steps you need to take if you want to achieve financial literacy and be financially successful in the future, what's the first thing you're going to do? Remember, one of the most important steps is the first one: consider your mindset around money and frame it to be both positive and constructive. This means forgiving yourself for your past mistakes, forming good spending habits, and being thankful for what you have.

The second action step involves setting your financial goals, which is also incredibly important. Your financial goals are the foundation on which you're going to build your future, after all! Once you establish your financial goals, you can move on to the third and fourth action steps: earning an active income and learning how to be disciplined with your money. This will likely take an adjustment period, but that's okay! Once you get into the swing of things, you'll be golden.

Once you start earning an active income, you can being saving up for your future. Saving, of course, takes time and discipline. It can be extremely helpful to budget wisely as well as get creative about finding inexpensive ways to spend your time. If you're able to set up some sort of passive income source for yourself, that's also an excellent way to save money!

When you feel like you've got your debts and finances under control, you should consider investing your money. Although investing can be risky, it can also be a great way to make more than enough money to save up for your future. Just be sure to make smart choices when making investments. Don't set unrealistic expectations or trust the wrong people.

Finally, regular financial reviews are incredibly important and necessary. Life can be unpredictable, so it's crucial to examine and reevaluate your finances and budget from time to time. I recommend reviewing your financial goals and budget at least every three months, but you can start with monthly financial reviews if that works better for you.

If you stick with the action steps discussed in this book, you should have no trouble achieving your financial goals. I encourage you to use the knowledge and momentum you've gained from reading this book and start planning out your financial future right away. Remember that if you're currently struggling with debt, there are ways you can dig yourself out of it if you're willing to put in a little grit and determination. Just think of Amanda Chatel's story! The choices you make now will determine your financial future. Keep chasing that dream home, that education, and that debt-free life. Your financial future is in your hands and it's up to you to mold it into something wonderful!

I hope you enjoyed reading this book and that it's given you some comprehensive guidance on how to live your best life as a financially savvy young adult. If you left a review, it would mean the world to me, as reviews from readers like you make all the difference. I wish you luck with your financial goals! Remember: you've got this.

RESOURCES

Dantus –, C.-R. (2019, June 5). *Budgeting: How to create a budget and stick with it*. Consumer Financial Protection Bureau. Retrieved March 21, 2023, from https://www.consumerfinance.gov/about-us/blog/budgeting-how-to-create-a-budget-and-stick-with-it/

5 Mistakes to Avoid When Setting Financial Goals. Netspend. (n.d.). Retrieved March 21, 2023, from https://www.netspend.com/blog/5-mistakes-to-avoid-when-setting-financial-goals

54 ways to save money. America Saves. (n.d.). Retrieved March 21, 2023, from https://americasaves.org/resource-center/insights/54-ways-to-save-money/

Baker, B. (n.d.). *6 best investments for beginners*. Bankrate. Retrieved March 21, 2023, from https://www.bankrate.com/investing/best-investments-for-beginners/

Beattie, A. (2023, March 11). *How to get out of debt in 8 steps*. Investopedia. Retrieved March 21, 2023, from https://www.investopedia.com/personal-finance/digging-out-of-debt/

Bieber, C. (2021, July 17). *6 tips for setting effective financial goals*. The Motley Fool. Retrieved March 21, 2023, from https://www.fool.com/the-ascent/banks/articles/6-tips-setting-effective-financial-goals/

Chatel, A. (2017, December 7). *I filed for bankruptcy at 23*. HuffPost. Retrieved March 21, 2023, from https://www.huffpost.com/entry/i-filed-bankruptcy-at-23_b_1553883

Dhawan, S. (n.d.). *How goal-setting helps plan your finances*. The Economic Times. Retrieved March 21, 2023, from https://economictimes.indiatimes.com/tdmc/your-money/how-goal-setting-helps-plan-your-finances/articleshow/51893734.cms

Financial tips: Six steps to creating a positive money mindset. Happy State Bank. (2022, June 1). Retrieved March 21, 2023, from https://www.

happybank.com/resources/six-steps-to-creating-a-positive-money-mindset

Fontinelle, A. (2023, March 15). *The biggest financial hurdles young people face*. Investopedia. Retrieved March 21, 2023, from https://www.investopedia.com/financial-edge/0712/the-biggest-financial-hurdles-young-people-face.aspx

Fry, S. (n.d.). *A financial success story to show how you can live within your means* ... Retrieved March 21, 2023, from https://financialpost.com/personal-finance/debt/household-makeover-financial-success-story-how-you-can-live-within-your-means

Goldman, A. (n.d.). *Investing 101 for beginners: How to start: Wealthsimple*. Wealthsimple. Retrieved March 21, 2023, from https://www.wealthsimple.com/en-ca/learn/investing-basics

Healthy spending: UCF Office of Student Financial Assistance. UCF Financial Aid. (2020, February 26). Retrieved March 21, 2023, from https://www.ucf.edu/financial-aid/financial-literacy/spending/

How a young Warren Buffett started his fortune. Net Net Hunter. (2020, December 31). Retrieved March 21, 2023, from https://www.netnethunter.com/how-young-warren-buffett-started-his-fortune/

How to build an emergency fund: Manulife plan & learn. How to build an emergency fund | Manulife Plan & Learn. (n.d.). Retrieved March 21, 2023, from https://www.manulife.ca/personal/plan-and-learn/healthy-finances/saving/how-to-build-an-emergency-fund.html

How to stay out of debt: 7 simple tips. Tally. (2022, September 15). Retrieved March 21, 2023, from https://www.meettally.com/blog/how-to-stay-out-of-debt

How to tell if you're financially responsible. Latitude Financial. (n.d.). Retrieved March 21, 2023, from https://www.latitudefinancial.com.au/life-done-better/are-you-financially-responsible.html

Hunt, J. (2021, April 20). *Financial goals feel unrealistic? here's what to do*. Credit Counselling Society. Retrieved March 21, 2023, from https://nomoredebts.org/blog/manage-money-better/financial-goals-feel-unrealistic

Investing & saving through life's stages. Merrill Edge. (n.d.). Retrieved March 21, 2023, from https://www.merrilledge.com/article/invest

ing-through-lifes-stages

Kagan, J. (2022, April 12). *What is active income?* Investopedia. Retrieved March 21, 2023, from https://www.investopedia.com/terms/a/activeincome.asp

Lane, C. (2021, November 24). *How students can find a job with no experience.* Top Universities. Retrieved March 21, 2023, from https://www.topuniversities.com/student-info/careers-advice/how-students-can-find-job-no-experience

LearnVest. (2014, January 10). *How I achieved my biggest money goal: 4 inspirational stories.* Forbes. Retrieved March 21, 2023, from https://www.forbes.com/sites/learnvest/2014/01/10/how-i-achieved-my-biggest-money-goal-4-inspirational-stories/?sh=10a8864b101a

Maranjian, S. (2019, March 20). *20 common beginner investor mistakes -- and how to avoid them.* The Motley Fool. Retrieved March 21, 2023, from https://www.fool.com/retirement/beginner-investor-mistakes-how-to-avoid.aspx

Meyers, S. (2021, July 6). *6 amazing benefits of earning a passive income.* Passive Storage Investing. Retrieved March 21, 2023, from https://passivestorageinvesting.com/6-amazing-benefits-of-earning-a-passive-income/

Moduet. (2022, June 14). *Why it's important for young people to have part-time jobs.* CWED. Retrieved March 21, 2023, from https://workethic.org/2018/09/19/why-its-important-for-young-people-to-have-part-time-jobs/

Moorhouse, C. (2022, March 3). *The importance of regular financial reviews.* Rhodes Wealth Management. Retrieved March 21, 2023, from https://rhodeswealthmanagement.co.uk/blog/the-importance-of-regular-financial-reviews/

Obdadmin. (2020, April 3). *The importance of saving at a young age.* 3RC. Retrieved March 21, 2023, from https://3rc.co.za/the-importance-of-saving-at-a-young-age/

Reddy, C. (2020, June 8). *21 very important things you learn on your first job.* Wisestep. Retrieved March 21, 2023, from https://content.wisestep.com/learn-first-job/

Royal, J. (n.d.). *23 passive income ideas to help you make money in 2023.*

Bankrate. Retrieved March 21, 2023, from https://www.bankrate.com/investing/passive-income-ideas/

Sabrina. (2021, May 31). *Home*. Finance Over Fifty. Retrieved March 21, 2023, from https://financeoverfifty.com/

Short-term thinking vs long-term vision - The Syndicate Group. The Syndicate Group. (n.d.). Retrieved March 21, 2023, from https://syndicategroup.com/short-term-thinking-vs-long-term-vision/

Volpe, E. (2021, October 20). *Financial goals: How do you stick to them?* Money Federal Credit Union. Retrieved March 21, 2023, from https://moneyfcu.org/how-often-should-you-review-financial-goals/

What is budgeting and why is it important? My Money Coach. (n.d.). Retrieved March 21, 2023, from https://www.mymoneycoach.ca/budgeting/what-is-a-budget-planning-forecasting

What is passive income? Ultimate Guide with examples. Shopify. (2022, October 6). Retrieved March 21, 2023, from https://www.shopify.com/ca/blog/passive-income

What you need to know about active income vs. passive income. Metrobank. (n.d.). Retrieved March 21, 2023, from https://www.metrobank.com.ph/articles/learn/active-vs-passive-income-basics

Why it pays to manage your money. Success at school. (n.d.). Retrieved March 21, 2023, from https://successatschool.org/advicedetails/859/why-it-pays-to-manage-your-money

Made in the USA
Coppell, TX
06 August 2024

35651716R00098